Mary Thompson

The Best of woman Fashion Knitting

NOTE

The photographs on pages 12
and 39 are printed back to front.
As a result, the cable patterns in
the sweater photographed on
page 39 appear in reverse.

Grafton Books
A Division of the Collins Publishing Group
8 Grafton Street, London W1X 3LA

Published by Grafton Books 1987

*British Library Cataloguing in Publication
Data*

Griffiths, Melody
The best of Woman fashion knitting.
1. Knitting – Patterns
I. Title
746.43′2041 TT820

ISBN 0-246-13197-7

Printed in Italy by New Interlitho spa, Milan

The Best of woman Fashion Knitting

Melody Griffiths

GRAFTON BOOKS
A Division of the Collins Publishing Group

LONDON GLASGOW
TORONTO SYDNEY AUCKLAND

Contents

Introduction

Knitting is a traditional craft that's rapidly becoming a modern art. I'm constantly amazed by the immense variety of effects that can be achieved with those two simple stitches – knit and purl. There are so many beautiful yarns to choose from too – soft wool, luxurious mohair, smooth cotton and clever mixtures of natural and man-made fibres. And the fascinating thing about knitting is the way that you create not just a fabric but also the shape of the garment at the same time.

But for most people the problem is finding the right design to make.

Every week in *Woman* magazine we feature knitting patterns that we hope will solve this problem. And we receive hundreds of letters asking for copies of patterns that have been lost or worn out with being knitted so many times.

So here, collected together in one book, are all your favourite designs from cool sophisticated classics and warm outdoor sweaters to colourful motif knits and woven-look woollies. Some look effective but are surprisingly easy to knit. Others are more challenging but nothing beats the satisfaction of being able to say, 'Yes, I made it myself.'

I do hope that you enjoy knitting these designs as much as I have enjoyed choosing them.

Melody Griffiths

Abbreviations

K = knit; p = purl; sts = stitches; s st = stocking stitch; g st = garter stitch; rev = reverse; m st = moss stitch; beg = begin; rep = repeat; tog = together; lp(s) = loop(s); yfd = yarn forward; ybk = yarn back; ytf = yarn to front; yrn = yarn round needle; tbl = through back of loop(s); skpo = slip 1, knit 1, pass slipped stitch over; psso = pass slipped stitch over; sppo = slip 1, purl 1, pass slipped stitch over; c = cable; c 3l = cable 3 left; c 3r = cable 3 right; c 4l = cable 4 left; c 4r = cable 4 right; inc = increase in next stitch; sl = slip; dec = decrease; m 1 = make 1; cont = continue; alt = alternate; foll = following; rem = remain; meas = measures; inst = instructions; s 1 = sequin 1; ch = chain; k1b = knit 1 below; t2l = twist 2 left; t2r = twist 2 right; patt = pattern.

Note.– Where more than one size is given, instructions are for smallest size with larger sizes in brackets.

At the beginning of each pattern we give the actual measurements as well as a 'to fit' size that indicates the amount of movement room that we think is right for that particular garment. Do look at these measurements carefully – you may choose to make a smaller size for a slimmer fit if you wish. Often the biggest size will fit size 16 and above.

We also give the tension. *Please, please* check your tension before starting to knit. It doesn't mean that there is anything in the least bit wrong with your knitting if you have to change your needle size from the recommended one – it just means that the tension the designer used was looser or tighter than yours. If you don't check – and change needles if necessary – how can you expect to achieve the same result?

Country comfort

et's start with one of the things that knitting does best – keeping you warm! But just because these sweaters and jackets are comfortable and keep out the cold doesn't mean that they lack style. Just take a closer look at these casual cables and rugged textures in earthy naturals, moody blues and country greens. If you are the kind of knitter who reaches for the needles as autumn approaches, these designs are definitely for you.

PLOUGHED EARTH

Moody blue

Summer cover-up or winter warmer – our textured jacket and roomy sweater have stylish cable and bobble stitches on the sleeves.

JACKET

MATERIALS: 20 (21:21) 50g balls Lister Pure Wool Aran; 3¾mm (No 9) and 4½mm (No 7) knitting needles; cable needle; 7 buttons.

Measurements: To fit 86 (91:97) cm, 34 (36:38) inch bust – actual meas, 99 (105:110) cm; length, 67 (69:72) cm; sleeve, 49 cm.

Tension: Over broken rib patt, 22 sts to 10 cm and 16 rows (4 patts) to 6 cm.

Abbreviations: See page 7.

BACK: With 3¾mm needles cast on 95 (101:107) sts. Work 15 (17:19) rows k 1, p 1 rib. **Inc row.** Rib 2 (5:1), * inc, rib 5 (5:6); rep from * to last 3 (6:1) sts, inc, rib 2 (5:0). 111 (117:123) sts. Change to 4½mm needles. Patt thus:
1st and 2nd rows. K. **3rd row.** P 1, (k 1, p 1) to end. **4th row.** K 1, (p 1, k 1) to end. These 4 rows form broken rib patt. Rep them 19 times more, then rep 1st and 2nd rows again.
Armhole Shaping: Cast off 6 sts at beg of next 2 rows **. Patt 62 (66:70) rows.
Shoulder Shaping: Cast off 8 (9:10) sts at beg of next 4 rows and 9 sts at beg of foll 2 rows. Patt 14 rows on rem 49 (51:53) sts for back extension. Cast off.

RIGHT FRONT: With 3¾mm needles cast on 45 (49:51) sts. Rib 15 (17:19) rows as back. **Inc row.** Rib 1 (3:4) sts, (inc, rib 5) 7 times, inc, rib 1 (3:4). 53 (57:59) sts. Change to 4½mm needles ***. Patt 16 rows as back, ending with a wrong side row.
Pocket Opening: Next row. Patt 35 (39:41), turn. Cont on these sts only. **Next row.** Cast on 7 sts for pocket border, k these 7 sts, patt to end. Working inner 7 sts in g st, patt 37 rows. **Next row.** Cast off 7 pocket border sts, patt to end. Patt 1 row. Leave sts on a spare needle. Rejoin yarn to inner end of rem 18 sts, cast on 23 sts for pocket lining, patt these 41 sts. Patt 39 rows. **Next row.** Cast off 23, patt to end. **Next row.** Patt to end, then patt 35 (39:41) sts from spare needle. 53 (57:59) sts. Patt 25 rows.
Armhole Shaping: Cast off 6 sts at beg of next row. Patt 56 (60:64) rows.
Neck Shaping: Cast off 13 (15:15) sts at beg of next row. Cast off 3 sts at beg of foll 3 alt rows.
Shoulder Shaping: Cast off 8 (9:10) sts at beg of next and foll alt row. Work 1 row. Cast off 9 sts.

LEFT FRONT: As right to ***. Patt 15 rows, ending with a right side row. Complete as right front from pocket opening.

SLEEVES: With 3¾mm needles cast on 49 (51:53) sts. Rib 15 rows as back. **Inc row.** Rib 0 (0:2), * inc, rib 5 (4:3); rep from * to last 1 (1:3) sts, inc, rib 0 (0:2). 58 (62:66) sts. Change to 4½mm needles and cont in patt from chart thus: **1st row** (right side). K 15 (17:19), reading chart from right to left, patt 28 sts of 1st row, k 15 (17:19). **2nd row.** K 15 (17:19), reading chart from left to right, patt 28 sts of 2nd row, k 15 (17:19). Now cont working each row of chart at centre, working sts at each end of every row in broken rib patt as back, inc 1 st each end of next and every foll 4th row until there are 90 (94:98) sts, then inc 1 st each end of every 3rd row until there are 124 (128:132) sts. Work 6 rows straight. **Next row.** Cast off 48 (50:52), patt centre 28 sts, cast off rem 48 (50:52). Break yarn. With wrong side facing, rejoin yarn and cont on centre 28 sts for saddle shoulder until 12th (2nd : 6th) row of 13th (14th:14th) chart patt from beg has been worked. Cast off.

FRONT BANDS: With 3¾mm needles cast on 8 sts for buttonhole band. Work 8 rows g st. **Buttonhole row.** K 3, cast off 2, k 3. **Next row.** K 3, cast on 2, k 3. Cont in g st and work 22 (23:24) rows, then rep 2 buttonhole rows. Rep last 24 (25:26) rows 5 times more. K 4 rows. Cast off. Work button band to match, omitting buttonholes.

NECKBAND: Join shoulders of back and fronts to sides of saddle shoulders of sleeves, then set side edges of 14-row back extension to 12 sts of cast-off edge of saddle shoulders. With right side facing, using 3¾mm needles k up 117 (123:125) sts around neck. Work 16 rows k 1, p 1 rib. K 1 row. Rib 16 rows. Cast off.

MAKING UP: Press lightly. Sew in

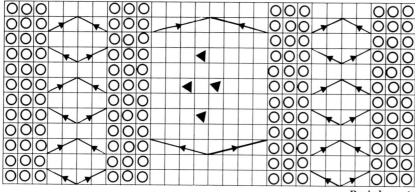

Begin here ▲

⊙ P on right side; k on wrong.

☐ K on right side; p on wrong.

Sl 1 st on to cable needle, leave at back, k 1, k st from cable needle.

Sl 1 st on to cable needle, leave at front, k 1, k st from cable needle.

◀ Pick up loop between needles before this st and k 1, (p 1, k 1) twice into loop, turn, k 5, turn, p 5, pass 2nd, 3rd, 4th and 5th sts over 1st and off needle; sl rem loop on to left-hand needle and k 2 tog tbl with this st.

Sl 2 sts on to cable needle, leave at back, k 2, k sts from cable needle.

Sl 2 sts on to cable needle, leave at front, k 2, k sts from cable needle.

remainder of sleeves, setting last 7 rows of sides of sleeves to cast-off groups at underarms. Join side and sleeve seams. Omitting ends of neckband, sew on front bands with cast-off edges to top. Fold neckband in half to wrong side and sew down; neaten ends. Sew on buttons. Sew down pocket linings and ends of pocket borders.

SWEATER

MATERIALS: Hayfield Brig Aran Pure New Wool is no longer available in blue, we suggest using 20 (21:21) 50g balls Sunbeam Aran Knit; 3¾mm (No 9) and 4½mm (No 7) knitting needles; cable needle.

Measurements: To fit 86 (91:97) cm, 34 (36:38) inch bust – actual meas, 99 (105:110) cm; length, 67 (69:72) cm; sleeve, 49 cm.

Tension: Over broken rib patt, 22 sts to 10cm and 16 rows (4 patts) to 6cm.

Abbreviations: See page 7.

BACK: As back of Moody Blue jacket.

FRONT: As back of Moody Blue jacket to **. Patt 54 (58:62) rows straight.

Neck Shaping: Next row. Patt 30 (32:34), cast off centre 39 (41:43) sts, patt 30 (32:34). Cont on last sts only and dec 1 st at neck edge on next 5 rows. Work 3 rows straight.

Shoulder Shaping: Cast off 8 (9:10) sts at beg of next and foll alt row. Work 1 row. Cast off 9 sts. With wrong side facing, rejoin yarn and work other side to match.

SLEEVES: As sleeves of Moody Blue jacket.

NECKBAND: Join both front and right back shoulders to saddle shoulders of sleeves in the same way as given for Moody Blue jacket. With right side facing, using 3¾mm needles and beg at 13th st from end of cast-off edge of left saddle shoulder (first 12 sts for back extension seam), k up 120 (124:128) sts around neck. Work 8 rows k 1, p 1 rib. K 1 row. Rib 8 rows. Cast off.

MAKING UP: Press lightly. Join left back shoulder extension seam and neckband. Sew in remainder of sleeves, setting last 7 rows at sides of sleeves to cast-off groups at underarms. Join side and sleeve seams. Fold neckband in half to wrong side and catch stitch.

MOODY BLUE JACKET

MOODY BLUE SWEATER

Bluestone

Casual, tweedy and studded with bobbles – this baggy
sweater is perfect with jeans.

MATERIALS: Sunbeam Aran Tweed:
18 (20:21) 50g balls main colour blue
(A). Sunbeam Aran Knit: 3 (50g) balls
2nd colour navy (B), 1 ball each 3rd colour denim (C), 4th colour light blue (D)
and 5th colour dark blue (E); 4½mm
(No 7) and 4mm (No 8) knitting
needles.

Measurements: To fit 86 (91:97) cm,
34 (36:38) inch bust – actual meas, 108
(114·5:121) cm; length, 64·5 (66:
68) cm; sleeve, 47 cm.

Tension: Over rev s st, 9 sts and 12 rows
to 5 cm.

Abbreviations: See page 7.

Note. – When working 9-bobble blocks
shown by symbols on diagram use a 350
cm length of yarn for colours other than
A. Work bobble sts only in this yarn and
leave it at end of each block on 2nd bobble row to be taken up again when 1st
row of block is repeated. Work each
group of 3 bobbles over 9 sts thus: **1st
row.** * With bobble colour k 1, p 1 and
k 1 all in next st, turn; p 1 and k 1 into
each of 3 sts, turn; (k 2 tog) 3 times *,
with A p next 3 sts of row, rep from * to
*, with A p next 3 sts, rep from * to *.
2nd row. Catching in bobble colour if in
contrast on 1st and every 4th st with A
(ytf, sl 1, p 2 tog, psso, k 3) twice, ytf,
sl 1, p 2 tog, psso.

BACK: With 4mm needles and B cast on
81 (85:89) sts. Work 2-colour rib thus:

1st row. With A k 1, (ybk, sl 1, k 1) to
end. **2nd row.** With A p 1, (ytf, sl 1, p 1)
to end. **3rd row.** With B ybk, sl 1, (ytf,
p 1, ybk, sl 1) to end. **4th row.** With B
ytf, sl 1, (ybk, k 1, ytf, sl 1) to end. These
4 rows form rib*. Rep them 7 times
more. Cont with A. **Inc row** (right side).
K 6 (4:1), (inc, k 3) to last 3 (1:0) sts, k
3 (1:0). 99 (105:111) sts. Change to
4½mm needles and beg k, work 11
(15:19) rows rev s st. Now read note at
beg and work 9-bobble block patt, referring to diagram, thus: ** **1st row**
(right side). P 9 (12:15), (in key colour
work 3 bobbles as given in note, p 15) 3
times, in key colour work 3 bobbles, p 9
(12:15). **2nd row.** K 9 (12:15), (complete 3 bobbles as given in note, k 15) 3
times, complete 3 bobbles, k 9 (12:15).
Work 4 rows rev s st. Rep last 6 rows
once, then 1st and 2nd of these rows
again. This completes a 9-bobble block
band. Beg p, work 20 rows rev s st ***.
Still working colours for bobble blocks
as diagram, rep from ** to *** twice,
then work last band of 9-bobble blocks.
Work 10 rows rev s st.

Shoulder Shaping: Cast off 28 (31:34)
sts, p 43 and leave these sts on a st-
holder for back neck, cast off rem sts.

FRONT: As back to ***. Still working
colours for 9-bobble blocks as diagram,
rep from ** to *** once, then work 3rd
band of 9-bobble blocks. Work 16 rows

BACK and FRONT

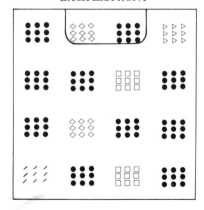

SLEEVES

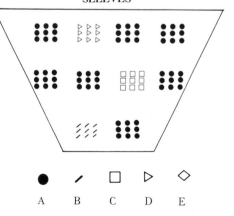

rev s st ending with a k row.

Neck Shaping: Next row. P 39 (42:45), cast off 21 sts, p 39 (42:45). Cont on last sts only. Dec 1 st at neck edge on next 3 rows, then while still dec at neck edge on next 8 rows and working 6 rows straight, work last 9-bobble block. Work 10 rows rev s st on rem 28 (31:34) sts. Cast off. Rejoin yarn and work other side of neck to match.

SLEEVES: With 4mm needles and B cast on 31 (33:35) sts. Work as back to *. Rep 4 rib rows 6 times more. Cont with A. **Inc row** (right side). K 6, inc in each of next 20 (22:24) sts, k 5. 51 (55:59) sts. Change to 4½mm needles. While inc 1 st each end of 2nd then 4th row, beg k, work 5 rows rev s st. Work bobble block patt referring to sleeve diagram. **Next row.** Inc, p 10 (12:14), in key colour work 9 sts of bobble block as given for back, p 15, in key colour work 9 sts of bobble block, p 10 (12:14), inc. Still inc each end of every alt row, complete 9-bobble blocks, then work 20 rows rev s st. 89 (93:97) sts.

Next row. Inc, p 3 (5:7), (in key colour work 9 sts of bobble block, p 15) 3 times, in key colour work 9 sts of bobble block, p 3 (5:7), inc. Still inc as set, complete 9-bobble blocks. 103 (107:111) sts. Now while inc 1 st each end of 4th and every foll 5th row, work 20 rows rev s st. 111 (115:119) sts.
Next row. P 15 (17:19), (in key colour work 9 sts of bobble block, p 15) 3 times, in key colour work 9 sts of bobble block, p 15 (17:19). Still inc each end of 3rd and every foll 5th row, complete 9-bobble blocks, then work 10 rows rev s st. 121 (125:129) sts. **Inc row.** P 6 (8:10), inc, (p 11, inc) 9 times, p 6 (8:10). 131 (135:139) sts. Change to 4mm needles. P 1 row. Rep 4 rib rows as at beg of back 4 times. Cast off with A.

NECKBAND: Matching sts, join 28 (31:34) sts of right shoulder. With right side facing, using 4mm needles and A k up 65 sts around front neck, then k 6, (p 2 tog, p 12) twice, p 2 tog, p 7 over sts of back neck. (105 sts) P 1 row, then rep 4 rib rows as at beg of back 6 times. Cast off with A.

MAKING UP: Press lightly avoiding 9-bobble blocks. Join left shoulder and neckband seam. Fold neckband in half to wrong side and catch stitch. Beg and ending 34 (35:36) cm from shoulders, sew cast-off edge of sleeves to sides. Join side and sleeve seams. With wrong side facing, catch stitch first rib row at top of sleeves to seam to form tuck on right side. Press seams.

Pebble

Knit husky wool into a chunky jacket with deep pockets and cable detail. It's a natural for town or country.

MATERIALS: Handweavers' Studio and Gallery Handspun Karakul is no longer available, we suggest using 2 kilos Handweavers' Studio 2 ply Berber, (see suppliers' list for address and telephone number on page 126; send stamp for shade fringe); 6mm (No 4) and 7mm (No 2) knitting needles; cable needle; 7 buttons.

Measurements: To fit 86 to 91 (97 to 102) cm, 34 to 36 (38 to 40) inch bust – actual meas, 107 (118) cm; length, 68 cm; sleeve, 49 cm.

Tension: 11 sts, 16 rows to 10 cm.

Abbreviations: See page 7.

BACK: With 6mm needles cast on 61 (67) sts. Work 6 cm k 1, p 1 rib. Change to 7mm needles. Beg k, cont in s st until work meas 45 cm.

Armhole Shaping: Cast off 12 (13) sts at beg of next 2 rows. 37 (41) sts. Cont straight until work meas 68 cm.

Shoulder Shaping: Cast off 7 (8) sts at beg of next 2 rows. Leave rem sts.

POCKET LININGS (2): With 7mm needles cast on 19 sts. Beg k, work 20 rows s st. Leave sts on a st-holder.

LEFT FRONT: With 6mm needles cast on 29 (31) sts. Rib 6 cm as back and *for 2nd size only,* inc 1 st at end of last of these rows. 29 (32) sts. Change to 7mm needles. Beg k, cont in s st until work meas 19 cm, ending p. **Pocket opening row.** K 5 (7), sl next 19 sts on to a st-holder, with right side facing k sts of one pocket lining, k 5 (6). Cont straight until work meas 45 cm, ending p.

Armhole Shaping: Cast off 12 (13) sts at beg of next row. Cont straight until work meas 62 cm, ending k.

Neck Shaping: Cast off 6 (7) sts at beg of next row. Dec 1 st at neck edge on next 4 rows. Work 4 rows. Cast off.

RIGHT FRONT: As left, reversing pocket opening row and all shapings.

LEFT SLEEVE: Beg at one edge of sleeve seam. With 7mm needles cast on 60 (61) sts. **1st row.** K *. **2nd row.** P 34 (35), (k 2, p 4) 4 times, k 2. Rep 1st and

2nd rows once more. **5th row.** (K 2, sl next 2 sts on to cable needle and leave at front of work, k next 2 sts, k 2 sts from cable needle) 4 times, k 36 (37). **6th row.** As 2nd. These 6 rows form patt. Patt until work meas 49 cm over s st from beg, ending with a 6th patt row. Cast off loosely.

RIGHT SLEEVE: As left to *. **2nd row.** K 2, (p 4, k 2) 4 times, p 34 (35). Rep 1st and 2nd rows once more. **5th row.** K 36 (37), (sl next 2 sts on to cable needle and leave at back of work, k next 2 sts, k 2 sts from cable needle, k 2) 4 times. **6th row.** As 2nd. These 6 rows form patt. Complete as left sleeve.

CUFFS: With right side facing, using 6mm needles k up 41 sts across plain end of sleeve. Rib 16 cm as back welt. Cast off.

NECKBAND: Join shoulder seams. With right side facing, using 6mm needles k up 17 (18) sts up right side of front, k back neck sts, k up 17 (18) sts

down left side of front. 57 (61) sts. Rib 13 rows. Cast off ribwise.

POCKET TOPS: With right side facing, sl sts of pocket on to 6mm needles. Rib 4 rows as back welt. Cast off ribwise.

FRONT BANDS: With 6mm needles cast on 7 sts. **1st row.** K 2, (p 1, k 1) to last st, k 1. **2nd row.** K 1, (p 1, k 1) to end. Rep last 2 rows once more. **Buttonhole row.** Rib 3, cast off 1 st, rib 3. **Next row.** Rib 3, cast on 1 st, rib 3. Cont in rib, making 6 more buttonholes 10 cm apart (measure from base of previous buttonhole, stretching rib slightly). Rib 4 rows. Cast off ribwise. Work other band, omitting buttonholes.

MAKING UP: Press work. Setting 11 (12) cm at sides of sleeves to cast-off groups at armholes, sew in sleeves. Join side and sleeve seams. Fold neckband and cuffs in half to wrong side and catch stitch. Sew down pocket linings and ends of pocket tops. Sew on front bands and buttons. Press seams.

Evergreen moss

Choose this chunky cardigan in wide twisted rib for simplicity and comfort.

MATERIALS: 8 (9) 100g balls Scotnord Alafoss Hespu-Lopi; 6½mm (No 3) and 7mm (No 2) knitting needles; 5 buttons; shoulder pads (optional).

Measurements: To fit 81 to 86 (91 to 97) cm, 32 to 34 (36 to 38) inch bust – actual meas, 102 (110) cm; length, 71 (72) cm; sleeve, 40 cm.

Tension: 16 sts (unstretched) to 11 cm; 17 rows to 10 cm.

BACK: With 6½mm needles cast on 75 (79) sts. Beg 1st row p 1 tbl, work 8 rows k 1 tbl, p 1 tbl rib, inc 1 st each end of last row. Change to 7mm needles. Patt thus: **1st row** (right side). P 2, (k 1 tbl, p 3) to end, ending last rep p 2. **2nd row.** K 2, (p 1 tbl, k 3) to end, ending last rep k 2 *. These 2 rows form patt. Cont until work meas 43 cm from beg.

Armhole Shaping: Cast off 5 sts at beg of next 2 rows. Patt straight until work meas 69 (70) cm from beg, ending with a wrong side row.

Neck Shaping: Next row. Patt 26 (27), cast off 15 (17), patt 26 (27). Cont on last set of sts only. Cast off 5 sts at beg of foll alt row. Patt 1 row. Cast off. Rejoin yarn at inner end of rem sts and complete other side to match.

POCKET LININGS (2): With 7mm needles cast on 18 sts. Beg k, work 19 cm s st, ending k. **Inc row.** P 1, (inc, p 3) to last st, inc. Leave 23 sts on a st-holder.

LEFT FRONT: With 6½mm needles cast on 35 (39) sts. Work as back to *. Patt until work meas 24 cm from beg, ending with a wrong side row. **Pocket opening row.** Patt 9, sl next 23 sts on a st-holder, patt 23 sts of one pocket lining, patt 5 (9). Cont straight until work meas 38 cm, ending with a right side row.

Front Shaping: Dec 1 st at beg of next row and at this edge on every foll 5th (4th) row until 35 (38) sts rem. *For 1st size only* work 3 rows.

Armhole Shaping: *For both sizes,* cast off 5 sts at beg of next row. Cont in patt, still dec 1 st at front edge on every 5th (4th) row as set until 21 (22) sts rem. Patt 6 rows. Cast off.

RIGHT FRONT: As left, reversing pocket opening row by reading from end to beg and reversing shapings.

SLEEVES: With 6½mm needles cast on 39 (43) sts. Work as back to *. Cont in patt, inc 1 st each end of next and every 3rd row until there are 81 (85) sts. Cont straight for 6 rows. Cast off loosely.

FRONT BAND: Join shoulder seams. With 6½mm needles cast on 6 sts. Beg 1st row k 1 tbl, rib 4 rows k 1 tbl, p 1 tbl rib. **Buttonhole row.** Rib 3, cast off 1, rib 2. **Next row.** Rib 2, cast on 1, rib 3. Rib 10 rows, then rep 2 buttonhole rows. Rep last 12 rows 3 times more. Cont in rib until band is long enough when slightly stretched to fit up both fronts and around back neck. Cast off ribwise.

POCKET TOPS: Sl sts on to 6½mm needle. With right side facing, beg 1st row p 1 tbl, rib 3 rows. Cast off ribwise.

MAKING UP: Press lightly. Setting 6 rows at sides of sleeves to cast-off sts at underarms, set in sleeves. Join side and sleeve seams. Sew on front band and buttons. Sew down pocket linings and ends of pocket tops. Sew in shoulder pads.

Fern

Brioche rib and cable, together with an unusual Aran weight wool, make the ideal outdoor sweater.

MATERIALS: 20 (22) 50g balls Viking Wools Falkland Islands Wool; 4½mm (No 7) and 5½mm (No 5) knitting needles; cable needle.

Measurements: To fit 86 to 91 (97 to 102) cm, 34 to 36 (38 to 40) inch bust – actual meas, 109 (126) cm; length, 65 cm; sleeve with turned back cuff, 44 cm.

Tension: 21 sts to 10 cm; 28 rows to 10·5 cm over rib; 14-st cable patt to 5 cm.

Abbreviations: See page 7.

BACK: With 4½mm needles cast on 119 (137) sts. **1st row.** P 2, * k 1, p 2; rep from * to end. **2nd row.** K 2, * p 1, k 2; rep from * to end. Rep these 2 rows for 12 cm, ending with 2nd row. **Inc row.** Rib 15 (24), (pick up strand lying between needles and k it tbl – referred to as m 1, rib 3) twice, m 1, * rib 15, (m 1, rib 3) twice, m 1; rep from * to last 14 (23) sts, rib to end. 134 (152) sts. Change to 5½mm needles. Cont in rib and cable patt thus: **1st row** (wrong side). K 2, (p 1, k 2) 4 (7) times, * (p 4, k 2) twice, (p 1, k 2) 4 (7) times; rep from * to end, ending last rep (p 1, k 2) 4 (7) times. **2nd row.** P 2, (k next st one row below st on needle letting sts above sl off in the usual way – referred to as k 1b, p 2) 4 (7) times, * (k 4, p 2) twice, (k 1b, p 2) 4 times; rep from * to end, ending last rep (k 1b, p 2) 4 (7) times. **3rd to 7th rows.** Rep 1st and 2nd rows twice then 1st row again. **8th row.** P 2, (k 1b, p 2) 4 (7) times, * sl 5 sts on cable needle and leave at front of work, k 4, p 1, then p 1, k 4 from cable needle, p 2, (k 1b, p 2) 4 times; rep from * to end, ending last rep (k 1b, p 2) 4 (7) times. **9th to 14th rows.** Rep 1st and 2nd rows 3 times. These 14 rows form patt **. Cont in patt until work meas 39 cm from beg, ending with 1st patt row.

Armhole Shaping: Cast off 6 (9) sts at beg of next 2 rows. 122 (134) sts. Cont straight until work meas 62 cm from beg, ending with 8th patt row.

Neck Shaping: Next row. Patt 51 (57) sts, turn. Cont on these sts only. Cast off 5 sts at beg of next and foll 2 alt rows. Work 1 row. Cast off 36 (42) sts. Rejoin yarn to inner end of rem sts, cast off centre 20 sts; work other side to match.

POCKET LININGS (2): With 5½mm needles cast on 28 sts. Work in s st for 11 cm, ending k. **Inc row.** (P 1, m 1) 3 times, p to last 3 sts, (m 1, p 1) 3 times. Leave 34 sts on a st-holder.

FRONT: Work as back to **. Patt 15 rows. **Pocket opening row.** Patt 14 (23) sts, * sl next 34 sts on a st-holder, patt 34 sts of one pocket lining *, patt 38 sts, rep from * to * once, patt to end. Cont as back until work meas 57 cm, ending with 7th patt row.

Neck Shaping: Next row. Patt 56 (62), turn. Cont on these sts only. Cast off 5 sts at beg of next and foll alt row, then cast off 2 sts at beg of every alt row until 36 (42) sts rem. Cont straight until work meas 65 cm from beg, ending with 1st patt row. Cast off. Rejoin yarn to inner end of rem sts, cast off centre 10 sts and work other side to match.

SLEEVES: With 4½mm needles cast on 53 sts. Rib 10 cm as back, ending with 2nd row. **Inc row.** (Rib 3, m 1) 3 times, * rib 15, (m 1, rib 3) twice, m 1; rep from * once more, rib 2. (62 sts) Change to 5½mm needles and patt thus: **1st row** (wrong side). K 2, * (p 4, k 2) twice, (p 1, k 2) 4 times; rep from * once, (p 4, k 2) twice. Cont in patt as set and *at the same time* inc 1 st each end of next and every foll 4th row until there are 116 sts, taking extra sts into rib at each side as they occur. Work 7 (11) rows straight, ending with 1st (5th) patt row. Cast off.

COLLAR: Join right shoulder seam. With right side facing, using 4½mm needles k up 25 sts down left side of front, 10 sts across centre front, 25 sts up right side of front, 12 sts down right side of back, 20 sts across centre back and 12 sts up left side of back. (104 sts) Beg and ending with 2nd row, rib as back for 5 cm. Now to reverse collar patt, beg with 2nd row again, cont in rib until collar meas 12 cm. Cast off ribwise.

POCKET TOPS: Sl pocket sts on to 4½mm needle. **Next row** (right side). P 1, k 1, (p 2, k 2 tog) twice, (p 2, k 1) 4 times, p 2, (k 2 tog, p 2) twice, k 1, p 1. Rib 4 cm as back. Cast off ribwise.

MAKING UP: Press very lightly. Join left shoulder and collar seam, reversing seam for final 7 cm of collar. Sew in sleeves setting 4 (6) cm at side of sleeves to cast-off groups at armholes. Join side and sleeve seams. Sew down ends of pocket tops and linings. Roll collar on to right side; fold back cuffs.

Ploughed earth

Natural shades of Welsh wool make a rough, tough sweater with masses of style.

MATERIALS: Cambrian Factory Welsh Aran (see suppliers' list for address and telephone number on page 126; send sae for shade fringe): 2 (400g) cones main colour grey (A) and 1 (350g) cone 2nd colour white (B) – sufficient for all sizes; 3¾mm (No 9) and 4½mm (No 7) knitting needles; cable needle.

Measurements: To fit 86 (91:97) cm, 34 (36:38) inch bust – actual meas, 100 (105:110) cm; length, 57 (58:59) cm; sleeve, 47 cm.

Tension: 12 sts to 5 cm; 30 rows to 13 cm over side panel patts.

Abbreviations: See page 7.

Note. –When working 2-colour pattern, do not strand yarns across work but use separate cones of yarn for each block of colour, twisting yarns together on wrong side when changing colour to avoid holes.

BACK: With 3¾mm needles and B cast on 86 (92:98) sts. Work 21 rows k 1, p 1 rib. **Inc row.** Rib 8 (11:14), pick up strand lying between needles and k it tbl – referred to as m 1, (rib 2, m 1) to last 8 (11:14) sts, rib to end. 122 (128:134) sts. Break off B. Change to 4½mm needles. Reading 1st and all right side rows of chart from right to left and 2nd and all wrong side rows from left to right, cont in patt thus: * **1st row.** For panel 1 k 57 (60:63) A, with B work 8 sts of 1st row of chart, for panel 2 k 57 (60:63) A. **2nd row.** For panel 2 with A (p 1, k 2) 19 (20:21) times, with B work 8 sts of 2nd row of chart, for panel 1 with A (k 2, p 1) 19 (20:21) times. **3rd row.** For panel 1 with A p 2, (taking needle in front of sts on left-hand needle k 2nd st, then p 1st st and sl both lps off tog – referred to as t 2 r, p 1) 18 (19:20) times, k 1, with B work 8 sts of 3rd row of chart, for panel 2 with A k 1, (p 1, taking needle behind sts on left-hand needle p into back of 2nd st, then k 1st st and sl both lps off needle tog – referred to as t 2 l) 18 (19:20) times, p 2. **4th row.** For panel 2 with A (k 2, p 1) 19 (20:21) times, with B work 8 sts of 4th row of chart, for panel 1 with A (p 1, k 2) 19 (20:21) times. **5th row.** For panel 1 with A (p 1, t 2 r) 19 (20:21) times, with B work 8

sts of 5th row of chart, for panel 2 with A (t 2 l, p 1) 19 (20:21) times. **6th row.** For panel 2 with A k 1, (p 1, k 2) 18 (19:20) times, p 1, k 1, with B work 8 sts of 6th row of chart, for panel 1 with A k 1, (p 1, k 2) 18 (19:20) times, p 1, k 1. **7th row.** For panel 1 with A (t 2 r, p 1) 19 (20:21) times, with B work 8 sts of 7th row of chart, for panel 2 with A (p 1, t 2

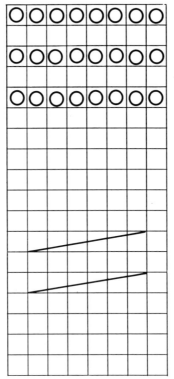

Begin here ▲

☐
K on right side; p on wrong.

⊙
K on wrong side.

Sl 3 sts on cable needle and leave at front, k next 3 sts, k 3 sts from cable needle.

l) 19 (20:21) times. Rep 2nd to 7th rows for patt of diagonal panel 1 and 2 at each side. Cont in side panel patts as set until 18-row centre panel patt from chart is completed, then work first 12 rows of chart again. Break off yarns. With B work 6 rows g st (shown on chart for centre panel patt), break off yarn *. Now to change direction of diagonal panels at each side, on odd-numbered (right side) rows work panel 2 first, then panel 1; on even-numbered (wrong side) rows work panel 1 first, then panel 2 and rep from * to * as now set once more. These 72 rows form patt **. Cont in patt until 14th (16th:18th) row of 7th chart patt at centre has been worked.

Shoulder Shaping: Cast off 14 (14:15) sts at beg of next 4 rows and 13 (15:15) sts at beg of foll 2 rows. Leave 40 (42:44) sts on a st-holder.

FRONT: As back to **. Cont in patt until 2nd (4th:6th) row of 7th chart patt has been worked.

Neck Shaping: Next row. Patt 51 (53:55) sts, turn. Cont on these sts only. Dec 1 st at neck edge on next 10 rows. Patt 1 row.

Shoulder Shaping: Cast off 14 (14:15) sts at beg of next and foll alt row. Patt 1 row. Cast off. Sl centre 20 (22:24) sts on a st-holder and work other side to match.

SLEEVES: With 3¾mm needles and B cast on 40 (42:44) sts. Work 13 rows k 1, p 1 rib. **Inc row.** Rib 6 (5:4), m 1, (rib 1, m 1) 27 (31:35) times, rib 7 (6:5). 68 (74:80) sts. Break off B. Change to 4½mm needles. Patt thus: **1st row** (right side). For panel 1 k 30 (33:36) A, with B work 8 sts of 1st row of chart, for panel 2 k 30 (33:36) A. Cont in patt as back on sts as set, inc 1 st each end of every 5th row until there are 104 (110:116) sts, taking extra sts at each side into patt panels. Patt until 12th row of 6th chart patt has been worked. Cast off loosely.

NECKBAND: Join right shoulder seam. With right side facing, using 3¾mm needles and B k up 22 sts down left side of front, k 20 (22:24) sts across centre, k up 22 sts up right side of front, k back neck sts. 104 (108:112) sts. Work 8 cm k 1, p 1 rib. Cast off ribwise.

MAKING UP: Press work lightly. Join left shoulder and neckband seam. Fold neckband in half to wrong side and catch stitch. Beg and ending 22 (23:24) cm from shoulder seams, sew sleeves on sides of back and front. Join side and sleeve seams. Press seams.

Chalk ridges

Combine keeping warm and looking feminine with this shapely sweater in rustic wool.

MATERIALS: Argyll Jacob Wool is no longer available, we suggest using Cambrian Factory Welsh Aran (see suppliers' list for address and telephone number on page 126; send sae for shade fringe): 2 (500g) cones main colour light (A), 50g each 2nd colour dark (B) and 3rd colour medium (C) – these quantities are sufficient for all 3 sizes; 4mm (No 8) and 5mm (No 6) knitting needles; cable needle.

Measurements: To fit 86 (91:97) cm, 34 (36:38) inch bust – actual meas, 100 (106:114) cm) length, 56 (61:65) cm; sleeve, 48 cm.

Tension: 18 sts and 25 rows to 10 cm over rev s st and s st.

Abbreviations: See page 7.

BACK: With 4mm needles and A cast on 86 (90:96) sts. Work 25 rows k 2, p 2 rib. **Inc row.** Rib 5 (3:6), pick up strand lying between needles and k into back of it – referred to as m 1, (rib 4, m 1) to last 5 (3:6) sts, rib 5 (3:6). 106 (112:118) sts. Read all instructions given with chart very carefully. Change to 5mm needles. Cont in patt from chart thus: **1st row** (wrong side). K 14 (17:20), reading 1st row of chart from left to right rep 26 sts of chart 3 times, k 14 (17:20). **2nd row.** P 14 (17:20), reading 2nd row of chart from right to left rep 26 sts of chart 3 times, p 14 (17:20). Now working sts at each end in rev s st, cont working 24-row chart as set, but on each row work 1st rep of chart as chart 1 patt (all A), centre rep of chart as chart 2 patt (B or C centre) and 3rd rep of chart as chart 1 patt (all A). Cont straight until 6th (12th:18th) row of 4th rep of chart patts has been worked, ending with a right side row.

Armhole Shaping: Cont working chart patts and cast off 6 sts at beg of next 2 rows. Dec 1 st at beg of every row until 78 (82:86) sts rem *. Cont straight until 8th (20th:8th) row of 6th (6th:7th) rep of chart patts has been worked.

Shoulder Shaping: Cast off 12 sts at beg of next 2 rows and 11 (12:13) sts at beg of foll 2 rows. Leave 32 (34:36) sts on a st-holder.

FRONT: As back to *. Cont straight until 12th (24th:12th) row of 5th (5th: 6th) rep of chart patts has been worked.

Neck Shaping: Next row (wrong side). Patt 30 (31:32), turn. Cont on these sts only. Dec 1 st at neck edge on every row until 23 (24:25) sts rem. Work 12 rows straight.

Shoulder Shaping: Cast off 12 sts at beg of next row. Work 1 row. Cast off. Sl centre 18 (20:22) sts on to a st-holder. Rejoin yarn at inner end of rem sts and complete other side of neck to match.

SLEEVES: With 4mm needles and A cast on 42 (44:48) sts. Rib 25 rows as back. **Inc row.** Rib 1 (2:4), m 1, (rib 3,

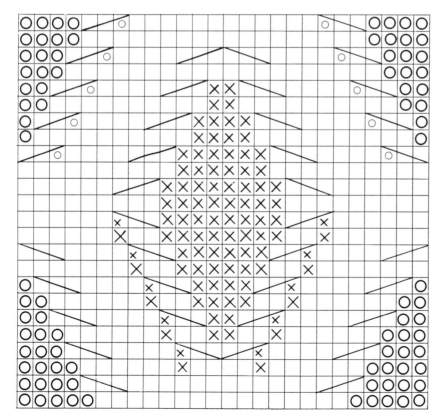

▲ Begin here

Only one chart is given. For chart 1 patt ignore X symbols and work these sts in rev s st with A. For chart 2 patt work X symbols in rev s st with B on 1st and alt reps and C on 2nd and alt reps, using a separate ball of A for each side of centre, twisting yarns on wrong side when changing colour to avoid holes.

P on right side; k on wrong.

K on right side; p on wrong.

Sl next st on to cable needle and leave at back, k 2, k st from cable needle.

Sl next 2 sts on to cable needle and leave at front, k 1, k sts from cable needle.

and

Sl next st on to cable needle and leave at back, k 2, p st from cable needle in colour of previous row.

and

Sl next 2 sts on to cable needle and leave at front, p 1 in colour of previous row, k sts from cable needle.

m 1) to last 2 (3:5) sts, rib 2 (3:5). 56 (58:62) sts. Change to 5mm needles. Beg k, cont in s st, inc 1 st each end of 3rd and every foll 14th row until there are 68 (72:76) sts. Cont straight until work meas 48 cm, ending p. To shape top cast off 6 sts at beg of next 2 rows. Dec 1 st each end of next and every foll 4th row until 48 sts rem. Dec 1 st each end of every alt row until 26 sts rem. P 1 row. Cast off.

NECKBAND: Join right shoulder. With 4mm needles and A k up 14 sts down left side of front, k centre front sts, k up 14 sts up right side of front and k back neck sts. 78 (82:86) sts. Work 27 rows k 2,

p 2 rib. Cast off loosely ribwise.

MAKING UP: Press work. Join left shoulder and neckband seam. Mark centre of cast-off group at top of sleeves, then make a 2-cm pleat at each side of this mark and secure by stitching edges tog. Set in sleeves. Join side and sleeve seams. Press seams.

Making shapes

very sweater has a shape, of course – but these are strong, stylish, definitive. There's everything from the feminine and fitted to the biggest ever batwing, from forties square shoulders to the simplest square sweater. And then there are three very unusual sweaters constructed in the entrelac technique – a fascinating way of knitting that made one reader say that all other knitting seemed rather ordinary after working our Aran Blocks pattern!

BASKETWEAVE

Forties mood

A strong shoulder line, a pretty stitch, zig-zag yoke detail – all add up to a stylish nostalgic sweater.

MATERIALS: 11 (50g) balls Robin Diamante; 3mm (No 11) and 3¾mm (No 9) knitting needles; shoulder pads.
Measurements: To fit 81 to 91 cm, 32 to 36 inch bust – actual meas, with rib unstretched, 78 cm; length, 48 cm; sleeve, 43 cm.
Tension: With rib unstretched, 15 sts to 5 cm; 12 rows to 4 cm.
Abbreviations: See page 7
Note. – When check counting sts count each "blister" as 1 st only.
BACK: With 3mm needles cast on 106 sts. Work 30 rows k 1, p 1 rib, inc 1 st at end of last row. (107 sts) Change to 3¾mm needles and cont in blister patt thus: **1st row.** P 2, (k 1, p 2) to end. **2nd row.** K 2, (p 1, k 2) to end. **3rd row.** P 2, * into next st (k 1, p 1) twice and k 1 thus making 5 sts from 1, p 2, k 1, p 2; rep from * to end, ending (k 1, p 1) twice and k 1 in next st, p 2. **4th row.** K 2, (p 5, k 2, p 1, k 2) to end, ending p 5, k 2. **5th row.** P 2, (k 2 tog, k 1, k 2 tog, p 2, k 1, p 2) to end, ending k 2 tog, k 1, k 2 tog, p 2. **6th row.** K 2, (p 3 tog, k 2, p 1, k 2) to end, ending p 3 tog, k 2. **7th row.** As 1st. **8th row.** As 2nd. **9th row.** P 2, * k 1, p 2, (k 1, p 1) twice and k 1 in next st, p 2; rep from * to end, ending k 1, p 2. **10th row.** K 2, (p 1, k 2, p 5, k 2) to end, ending p 1, k 2. **11th row.** P 2, (k 1, p 2, k 2 tog, k 1, k 2 tog, p 2) to end, ending k 1, p 2. **12th row.** K 2, (p 1, k 2, p 3 tog, k 2) to end, ending p 1, k 2. These 12 rows form patt. Cont in patt and inc 1 st each end of next and every foll 6th row until there are 119 sts. Cont straight until 6th row of 6th patt from beg has been worked.
Armhole Shaping: Note that st left on right-hand needle after cast-off group at beg of each row is not included in instructions for rest of row. When working patt sts, refer to note at beg. **1st row.** Cast off 5, p 2, (k 1, p 2) 4 times, * (k 1, p 1, pick up loop lying between needles and k into back of it – referred to as m 1, p 1) twice, (k 1, p 2) 6 times; rep from * 3 times, k 1, p 2. **2nd row.** Cast off 5, (k 2, p 1) 4 times, k 2, * p 1, (k 1, p 1) 4 times for rib, (k 2, p 1) 5 times, k 2; rep from * twice, rib 9, (k 2, p 1) 5 times. **3rd row.**

Cast off 4, patt 10, (rib 9, patt 17) 3 times, rib 9, patt 3, (p 2, k 1) 4 times. **4th row.** Cast off 4, patt 10 as set, (rib 9, patt 17) 3 times, rib 9, patt 3, (k 2, p 1) twice, k 2. **5th row.** Cast off 4, patt 6, (rib 9, patt 17) 3 times, rib 9, patt 11. **6th row.** Cast off 4, patt 6, (rib 9, patt 17) 3 times, rib 9, patt 7. **7th row.** Patt 4, (k 1, p 1, m 1, rib 11, m 1, p 1, k 1, patt 11) 3 times, k 1, p 1, m 1, rib 11, m 1, p 1, k 1, patt 4. **8th to 12th rows.** Patt 4, (rib 17, patt 11) 3 times, rib 17, patt 4. **13th row.** Rib 3, m 1, (rib 19, m 1, rib 2, patt 5, rib 2, m 1) 3 times, rib 19, m 1, rib 3. **14th to 18th rows.** Rib 26, (patt 5, rib 25) 3 times, k 1. **19th row.** (Rib 27, m 1, rib 3, m 1,) 3 times, rib 27. **20th row.** Rib to end. (123 sts)**. Rib 30 more rows.
Shoulder Shaping: Cast off 20 sts at beg of next 4 rows. Cast off 43 sts.
FRONT: As back to **. Rib 18 rows.
Neck Shaping: Next row. Rib 50 sts, turn. Cont on these sts only and dec 1 st at neck edge on every row until 40 sts rem. Rib 1 row.
Shoulder Shaping: Cast off 20 sts at beg of next and foll alt row. Cast off centre 23 sts. Complete other side of neck to match.
SLEEVES: With 3mm needles cast on 52 sts. Rib 30 rows as back, inc 1 st at end of last row. (53 sts) Change to 3¾mm needles and patt as back, inc 1 st each end of 13th row and every foll 8th row until there are 77 sts. Work 1 row, thus ending with 6th row of 9th patt. To shape top cast off 5 sts at beg of next 2 rows. Dec 1 st each end of next and every foll alt row until 21 sts rem. Cast off.
NECKBAND: Join right shoulder. With 3mm needles k up 96 sts around neck. Work 8 rows k 1, p 1 rib. Cast off loosely ribwise.
MAKING UP: Do not press. Join left shoulder and neckband seam. Join side and sleeve seams. Beg and ending at each end of cast-off edges of sleeve tops, make a small tuck down each shaped side edge of work and sew in place by stitching edges tog. Set in sleeves. Sew in shoulder pads.

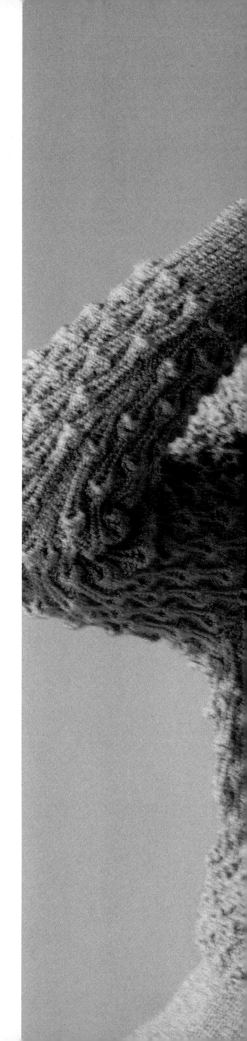

Slimline

Twisted ribs twine into cables then spread gently out to the shoulders of this clever, figure-flattering sweater.

MATERIALS: 22 (23) 25g hanks Rowan Lightweight Double Knitting Wool; 3¼mm (No 10) and 3¾mm (No 9) knitting needles; 3¼mm (No 10) circular knitting needle, 40 cm long; cable needle; shoulder pads.

Measurements: To fit 81 to 86 (91 to 97) cm, 32 to 34 (36 to 38) inch bust – actual meas, 88 (99) cm; length, 60 cm; sleeve, 38 cm.

Tension: Equivalent to 12 sts, 16 rows to 5 cm over s st; rib 11 and s st 7 to 5·5 cm.

Abbreviations: See page 7.

BACK: With 3¼mm needles cast on 147 (165) sts. **1st row.** P 1, (k 1 tbl, p 1) to end. **2nd row.** K 1, (p 1 tbl, k 1) to end *. Rep these 2 rows 4 times more. Change to 3¾mm needles. Rib patt thus: **1st rib row** (right side). P 5, (k 1 tbl, p 1) 5 times, k 1 tbl – referred to as rib 11, (p 7, rib 11) to last 5 sts, p 5. **2nd rib row.** K 5 (p 1 tbl, k 1) 5 times, p 1 tbl – referred to as rib 11, (k 7, rib 11) to last 5 sts, k 5. Rep last 2 rows until work meas 12 cm, ending with a wrong side row. **Dec row.** P 5, * k 1, (k 2 tog) 5 times, p 7; rep from * to end, ending last rep p 5. 107 (120) sts. Cable patt thus: **1st row** (wrong side). K 5, p 6, (k 7, p 6) to last 5 sts, k 5. **2nd row.** P 5, (sl next 3 sts on cable needle and leave at front of work, k 3, k sts from cable needle – referred to as c 6, p 7) to end, ending last rep p 5. **3rd row.** As 1st. **4th row.** P 5, (k 6, p 7) to end, ending last rep p 5. **5th row.** As 1st. **6th row.** As 4th. These 6 rows form patt. Cont until 3rd row of 10th cable patt has been worked. **Inc row** (right side). P 5, * k 1, (pick up strand lying between needles and p it tbl – referred to as m 1, k 1) 5 times, p 7; rep from * to end, ending last rep p 5. Work 2nd rib patt row once, then rep 1st and 2nd rib patt rows 18 times. ** **Inc row** (right side). P 5, (m 1, rib 11, m 1, p 7) to end, ending last rep p 5. **Next row.** K 6, (rib 11, k 9) to end, ending last rep k 6. **Next row.** P 6, (rib 11, p

9) to end, ending last rep p 6. Rep last 2 rows 17 times more, then 1st row again. **Inc row** (right side). P 6, (m 1, rib 11, m 1, p 9) to end, ending last rep p 6. **Next row.** K 7, (rib 11, k 11) to end, ending last rep k 7. **Next row.** P 7, (rib 11, p 11) to end, ending last rep p 7 ***. Rep last 2 rows 13 times more, then 1st of these rows again **.

Shoulder and Neck Shaping: Cast off 9 (11) sts at beg of next 6 rows. **Next row.** Cast off 9 (10), patt 37 (40), turn. Cont on these sts only. While casting off 4 sts at beg of next row and 3 sts at beg of foll 2 alt rows *at the same time* cast off 9 (10) sts at beg of foll 3 alt rows at shoulder. Sl centre 33 (35) sts on a st-holder, rejoin yarn at inner end and complete other side to match.

FRONT: As back to ***. Rep last 2 rows twice more, then 1st row again.

Neck Shaping: Next row. Patt 73 (83), turn. Cont on these sts only. Dec 1 st at neck edge on next 5 rows, then dec 1 st at same edge on every foll alt row until 63 (73) sts rem. Work 6 rows straight.

Shoulder Shaping: Cast off 9 (11) sts at beg of next and foll 2 alt rows, then cast off 9 (10) sts at beg of foll 4 alt rows. Sl centre 33 (35) sts on a st-holder, rejoin yarn at inner end and complete other side to match.

SLEEVES: With 3¼mm needles cast on 63 sts. Work as back to *. Rep these 2 rows 9 times more. **Inc row** (right side). P 1, m 1, p 2, m 1, (rib 1, m 1) twice, rib 3, (m 1, rib 1) twice, * (m 1, p 1) 3 times, m 1, (rib 1, m 1) twice, rib 3, (m 1, rib 1) twice; rep from * 4 times more, m 1, p 2, m 1, p 1. (111 sts). Change to 3¾mm needles. **Next row.** K 5, * p 1 tbl, (k 1, p 1 tbl) 5 times, k 7; rep from * to end, ending last rep k 5. Rep 1st and 2nd rib patt rows of back 18 times more. Work as back from ** to **. Cast off loosely.

NECKBAND: Join shoulder seams. With right side facing, using circular needle, beg at left shoulder seam and k up 32 sts down left side of front, patt centre sts, k up 32 sts up right side of front and 11 sts down right side of back, patt centre back sts, k up 11 sts up left side of back. 152 (156) sts. With right side facing cont in rounds and beg k 1 tbl, work 11 rounds k 1 tbl, p 1 rib. Cast off loosely ribwise.

MAKING UP: Press work lightly. Beg and ending 23 cm from shoulder seams, taking 1½ sts of back and front edges into seam, sew on sleeves. Taking 1½ sts from each edge into seams, join side and sleeve seams. Press seams lightly. Sew in shoulder pads.

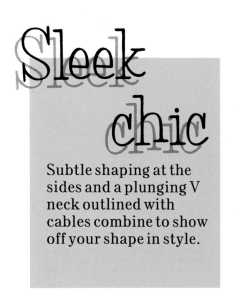

Sleek chic

Subtle shaping at the sides and a plunging V neck outlined with cables combine to show off your shape in style.

MATERIALS: 9 (10:10) 50g balls Patons Cotton Perlé; 3¼mm (No 10) and 4mm (No 8) knitting needles; 3¼mm (No 10) circular knitting needle, 60 cm long; cable needle; shoulder pads.

Measurements: To fit 86 (91:97) cm, 34 (36:38) inch bust closely – actual meas, 85 (90:96) cm; length, 53 (54·5:56) cm; sleeve, 42 cm.

Tension: 22 sts, 29 rows to 10 cm over rev s st; 20 sts of cable patt to 7 cm.

Abbreviations: See page 7.

BACK: With 3¼mm needles cast on 91 (97:103) sts. **1st row** (wrong side). (K 1 tbl, p 1) 4 (5:6) times, * k 2, (p 4, k 2) 3 times *, p 1, (k 1 tbl, p 1) 17 (18:19) times, rep from * to * again, (p 1, k 1 tbl) 4 (5:6) times. **2nd row.** (P 1, k 1 tbl) 4 (5:6) times, p 2, (* sl next 2 sts on cable needle and leave at front, k 2, k sts from cable needle* – referred to as c 4 l, p 2) 3 times, k 1 tbl, (p 1, k 1 tbl) 17 (18:19) times, p 2, (rep from * to * but leave sts at back – referred to as c 4 r, p 2) 3 times, (k 1 tbl, p 1) 4 (5:6) times. **3rd row.** As 1st. **4th row.** (P 1, k 1 tbl) 4 (5:6) times, * p 2, (k 4, p 2) 3 times *, k 1 tbl, (p 1, k 1 tbl) 17 (18:19) times, rep from * to * again, (k 1 tbl, p 1) 4 (5:6) times. These 4 rows form rib and cable patts. Cont until 8th cable patt from beg has been worked **. Change to 4mm needles. **Next row** (wrong side). K 5 (7:9), * rib 3, cable patt 20 as set, rib 3 *, k 29 (31:33), rep from * to * once, k 5 (7:9). **Next row.** P 5 (7:9), * rib 3, cable patt 20 as set, rib 3 *, p 29 (31:33), rep from * to * once, p 5 (7:9). Cont in rev s st, rib and cable patt as set for 5 rows more.

Side Shaping: Cont in patt as set, inc 1 st each end of next and every foll 10th row until there are 105 (111:117) sts, working extra sts in rev s st. Patt 5 (7:9) rows.

Armhole Shaping: Cast off 5 (6:7) sts at beg of next 2 rows. Dec 1 st each end of next 3 rows, then dec 1 st each end of foll 3 alt rows. 83 (87:91) sts. Work 41 (43:45) rows straight.

Shoulder Shaping: Cast off 10 sts at beg of next 4 rows and 9 (10:11) sts at beg of foll 2 rows. Leave rem 25 (27:29) sts on a st-holder.

FRONT: – With 3¼mm needles cast on 91 (95:103) sts. **1st row** (wrong side). (K 1 tbl, p 1) 10 (11:13) times, * k 2, (p 4, k 2) 3 times *, p 1, (k 1 tbl, p 1) 5 times, rep from * to * once, (p 1, k 1 tbl) 10 (11:13) times. **2nd row.** (P 1, k 1 tbl) 10 (11:13) times, p 2, (c 4 r, p 2) 3 times, k 1 tbl, (p 1, k 1 tbl) 5 times, p 2, (c 4 l, p 2) 3 times, (k 1 tbl, p 1) 10 (11:13) times. **3rd row.** As 1st. **4th row.** Rib 20 (22:26), * p 2, (k 4, p 2) 3 times *, rib 11, rep from * to * again, rib 20 (22:26). These 4 rows form rib and cable patt. Cont as back to ** and *for 2nd size only* inc 1 st each end of last of these rows. 91 (97:103) sts. Change to 4mm needles. Patt thus: **Next row.** K 17 (20:23), * rib 3, cable patt 20 as set, rib 11, cable patt 20 as set, rib 3, k 17 (20:23).

Front Shaping: Next row. P 17 (20:23), rib 3, cable patt 20, rib 4, k 1, turn. Cont on these sts only and work 1 st at neck edge k on every row. Patt 5 rows.

Side and Front Shaping: Shaping row. Inc, p 14 (17:20), p 2 tog, patt to end. Patt 9 rows, then rep shaping row again. Rep last 10 rows 5 times more. Work 5 (7:9) rows straight.

Armhole Shaping: While casting off 5 (6:7) sts at beg of next row and dec 1 st at this edge on next 3 rows, then 1 st on foll 3 alt rows *at the same time* dec 1 st at inner edge of cable patt on every 10th row as set until 29 (30:34) sts rem. *For 3rd size only* dec 1 st at inner edge of cable patt on every foll 8th row until 31 sts rem. *For all sizes,* work 7 (1:1) rows. **Shoulder Shaping:** Cast off 10 sts at beg of next and foll alt row. Work 1 row. Cast off. Sl centre st on a safety pin, rejoin yarn at inner end of rem sts and work other side to match, working c 4 l cable patt, and reversing shapings.

SLEEVES: *Right.* – With 3¼mm needles cast on 48 (52:56) sts. **1st row** (wrong side). (K 1 tbl, p 1) 7 (8:9) times, k 2, (p 4, k 2) 3 times, (p 1, k 1 tbl) 7 (8:9) times. **2nd row.** (P 1, k 1 tbl) 7 (8:9) times, p 2, (c 4 r, p 2) 3 times, (k 1 tbl, p 1) 7 (8:9) times. Cont in rib

SLEEK CHIC

and cable patt as set and work as back to **. **Inc row.** Rib 2 (4:6), (inc, rib 3) 3 times, patt 20, (rib 3, inc) 3 times, rib 2 (4:6). 54 (58:62) sts. Change to 4mm needles. Patt thus: **Next row.** P 14 (16:18), rib 3, cable patt 20, rib 3, p 14 (16:18). **Next row.** K 14 (16:18), rib 3, cable patt 20, rib 3, k 14 (16:18). Cont in patt as set, inc 1 st each end of next and every foll 6th row until there are 78 (82:86) sts, working extra sts in rev s st. Cont straight until work meas 43 cm from beg, ending with a 4th patt row.

To shape top cast off 5 (6:7) sts at beg of next 2 rows. Dec 1 st at beg of every row until 38 sts rem. Cast off 3 sts at beg of next 4 rows. Cast off. *Left.* – As right but work c 4 l cable patt instead of c 4 r cable patt.

NECKBAND: Join shoulder seams. With right side facing, using circular needle, beg at left shoulder seam and k up 90 (94:96) sts down left side of front, p st from safety pin, k up 90 (94:96) sts up right side of front, across back neck sts: p 3 (4:5), inc, (p 5, inc) 3 times, p 3 (4:5). 210 (220:226) sts. Cont in rounds thus: **1st round.** (K 1 tbl, p 1) to within 2 sts of centre st, skpo, p centre st, k 2 tog, (p 1, k 1 tbl) to last st, p 1. **2nd round.** (K 1, p 1 tbl) to within 3 sts of centre st, k 1, skpo, p centre st, k 2 tog, (k 1, p 1 tbl) to end. Cont in rib as set dec 1 st each side of centre st on foll 14 rounds. Cast off ribwise.

MAKING UP: Press lightly. Set in sleeves. Join side and sleeve seams. Press seams. Sew in shoulder pads.

Simply square

Two squares, emphasised by easy-to-work right angled stripes make the back and front of this striking sweater.

MATERIALS: Sirdar Majestic Double Knitting Wool is no longer available, we suggest using Sirdar Sovereign Double Knitting: 8 (9:9) 50g balls 1st colour light blue (A) and 6 (7:7) balls 2nd colour dark blue (B); 3¼mm (No 10) and 4mm (No 8) knitting needles.

Measurements: To fit 86 (91:97) cm, 34 (36:38) inch bust – actual meas, 97 (103:109) cm; length, 59 (62:65) cm; sleeve, 45 cm.

Tension: 11 sts, 22 rows to 5 cm.

Abbreviations: See page 7.

BACK AND FRONT alike: With 3¼mm needles and A cast on 103 (107:111) sts. Work 28 rows k 1, p 1 rib. **Inc row.**

Rib 11 (8:7), inc, * rib 19 (14:11), inc; rep from * 3 (5:7) times more, rib 11 (8:7), turn and cast on 108 (114:120) sts. 216 (228:240) sts. Change to 4mm needles. Cont in 2-row g st stripes. **1st row** (right side). With B k 106 (112:118), k 2 tog, k 2 tog tbl, k 106 (112:118). **2nd row.** With B k. **3rd row.** With A k 105 (111:117), k 2 tog, k 2 tog tbl, k 105 (111:117). **4th row.** With A k. These 4 rows form stripe patt. Cont in stripe patt, still shaping as set working 1 st less before and after decs on next and every foll alt row until 4 sts rem. **Next row.** K 4. **Next row.** K 2 tog, k 2 tog tbl. K 2 tog; fasten off.

SLEEVES: With 3¼mm needles and A cast on 51 (53:55) sts. Rib 28 rows as back. **Inc row.** Rib 3 (4:5), inc, (rib 4, inc) 9 times, rib 2 (3:4). 61 (63:65) sts. Change to 4mm needles. Working in g st stripes of 2 rows each B and A *at the same time* inc 1 st each end of 7th and every foll 6th row until there are 89 (93:97) sts. Cont straight until work meas 45 cm, ending with a wrong side row. Cast off loosely.

NECKBAND: Join one shoulder for 11 (11·5:12) cm from end. With right side facing, using 3¼mm needles and A beg 11 (11.5:12) cm from other end and k up 60 (61:62) sts across edge to seam, then 60 (61:62) sts across other edge to within 11 (11.5:12) cm of end. Work 10 rows k 1, p 1 rib. K 1 row (hemline). Rib 10 rows. Cast off loosely ribwise.

MAKING UP: Join rem shoulder and neckband seam. Fold neckband in half to wrong side and catch stitch. Beg and ending 20 (21:22) cm from shoulder seams, sew sleeves on sides of back and front. Join side and sleeve seams.

Big batwing

An easy, unrestricted shoulder line and a deep, deep armhole make this stylish batwing sweater a joy to relax in. The detail that looks like a cable is just a knitted cord threaded through holes.

MATERIALS: 14 (16) 50g balls Richard Poppleton Emmerdale Double Knitting; 3¼mm (No 10) knitting needles; a set of four 3¼mm (No 10) double-pointed knitting needles; a 4mm (No 8) circular knitting needle, 100 cm long.

Measurements: To fit 81 to 91 (91 to 102) cm, 32 to 36 (36 to 40) inch bust very loosely; centre back to cuff, 76 (77) cm; length, 67 (68) cm.

Tension: 13 sts, 16 rows to 5 cm.

Abbreviations: See page 7.

BACK AND SLEEVES: With 3¼mm needles cast on 111 (123) sts. Work 23 rows k 1, p 1 rib. **Inc row.** Rib 10 (3), (inc, rib 5) 16 (20) times, rib 5 (0). 127 (143) sts. Change to circular needle and work forward and back in rows.

1st row (right side). * Reading 1st row of chart 1 from right to left, rep 4 sts before dotted line 3 (4) times, work 2 sts beyond dotted line *; reading 1st row of chart 2 from right to left, work 8 sts before right-hand dotted line, rep 8 sts between dotted lines 11 (12) times, work 3 sts beyond left-hand dotted line; rep from * to * once more. **2nd row.** * Reading 2nd row of chart 1 from left to right, work 2 sts before dotted line, rep 4 sts beyond dotted line 3 (4) times *; reading 2nd row of chart 2 from left to right work 3 sts before left-hand dotted line, rep 8 sts between dotted lines 11 (12) times, work 8 sts beyond right-hand dotted line; rep from * to * once more. Work 3rd and 4th rows of charts in this way. While inc 1 st each end of next and every foll alt row work 5th to 8th rows of charts then rep 8 chart rows for patt, taking extra sts into additional reps of chart 1 patt at each end of work until there are 205 (221) sts. Inc 1 st each end of every row until there are 279 (295) sts. Cast on 10 (6) sts at beg of next 2 rows, 14 sts at beg of next 2 rows and 24 sts at beg of foll 2 rows. 375 (383) sts **. Patt straight until 8th (4th) row of 24th (25th) patt from beg has been worked and work meas 67 (68) cm.

Shoulder and Upper Sleeve Shaping: Cast off 163 (165) sts at beg of next 2 rows. Leave 49 (53) sts on a st-holder.

FRONT AND SLEEVES: As back to **. Patt straight until 2nd (6th) row of 21st patt from beg has been worked and work meas 58 (59) cm from beg, ending with a wrong side row.

Neck Shaping: Next row. Patt 177 (181) sts, turn. Cont on these sts only. Cast off 4 sts at beg of next row and 3 (4) sts at beg of foll 2 alt rows. Patt 1 row.

Dec 1 st at beg of next row and at this edge on every foll 3rd row until 163 (165) sts rem. Patt 13 rows. Cast off. Sl centre 21 sts on a st-holder and work to match other side.

NECKBAND: Join both shoulder and upper sleeve seams, matching cast-off sts. With right side facing, using 3¼mm double-pointed needles and spacing sts evenly over 3 needles, beg at left shoulder seam and k up 25 (27) sts down left side of front, k centre sts, k up 25 (27) sts up right side of front, k back neck sts. 120 (128) sts. Work 20 rows k 1, p 1 rib. Cast off loosely ribwise.

CUFFS: With right side facing, using 3¼mm needles k up 118 (126) sts across straight edge of sleeve. **1st row.** (P 2 tog) to end. 59 (63) sts. Work 10 rows k 1, p 1 rib. Cast off ribwise.

CORDS (2): *Hand Knitting.* – With two 3¼mm double-pointed needles cast on 3 sts. Cont thus: K 3, * do not turn but push sts along to other end of needle, draw up yarn tightly behind sts and k 3; rep from * until cord is 220 (230) cm long. Cast off tightly. *Machine Knitting or Knitting Nancy.* Work as instruction handbook to lengths given above.

MAKING UP: Do not press. Join side and sleeve seams. Fold neckband in half to wrong side and catch stitch. Press seams lightly. Lace cords through holes at each side of chart 2 patt thus: Beg above welt and bring cord to right side through 1st hole. Now cont Back Stitching through holes thus: Miss next hole, * take cord through next hole and back through missed hole to right side, then miss next free hole and rep from * over shoulder and down to last hole above welt. Sew down ends.

KEY FOR CHARTS 1 AND 2

☐ K on right side; p on wrong.

Ⓞ P on right side; k on wrong.

⊠ K 2 tog without slipping sts off left-hand needle, k 1st of these sts again and s1 both sts off in the usual way.

❯ Yarn round needle between sts.

❮ Make 1 by picking up strand between needles and purl it.

⊠ P 2 tog.

⟠ P 3 tog.

Chart 2

Chart 1

Begin here ▲   Begin here ▲

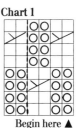

Basketweave

A clever way of knitting stocking stitch makes this sweater look as though it's made from woven strips.

MATERIALS: Sirdar Pullman is no longer available, we suggest using Sirdar Sovereign Chunky: 6 (50g) balls 1st colour navy (A), 5 balls 2nd colour red (B), 4 balls each 3rd colour green (C) and 4th colour blue (D); 5½mm (No 5) and 6½mm (No 3) knitting needles.

Measurements: To fit 86 to 97 cm, 34 to 38 inch bust – actual meas, 120 cm; length 60 cm; sleeve, 43 cm.

Tension: 7 sts to 5 cm; 13 rows to 7 cm.

Abbreviations: See page 7.

BACK AND FRONT ALIKE: With 5½mm needles and A cast on 50 sts. Work 10 cm k 1, p 1 rib. K 1 row (right side). Change to 6½mm needles, refer to diagram throughout and work thus:

1st Band. With A * p 2, turn and k 2; p 3, turn and k 3; p 4, turn and k 4; p 5, turn and k 5; p 6, turn and k 6; p 7, turn and k 7; p 8, turn and k 8; p 9, turn and k 9; p 10 and sl these 10 sts on a spare needle *. Cont working across rem sts. Rep from * to * to end, but leave last 10 sts on needle.

2nd Band. Change to B. ** With right side facing, cont thus: K 2, turn and p 2; inc in 1st st, skpo, turn and p 3; inc in 1st st, k 1, skpo, turn and p 4; inc in 1st st, k 2, skpo, turn and p 5; inc in 1st st, k 3, skpo, turn and p 6; inc in 1st st, k 4, skpo, turn and p 7; inc in 1st st, k 5, skpo, turn and p 8; inc in 1st st, k 6, skpo, turn and p 9; inc in 1st st, k 7,

skpo and sl these 10 sts on a st-holder. *** With right side facing, with B k up 10 sts down left-hand side of same section of previous band, turn and work over these and next group of sts on spare needle thus: (p 10, turn and k 9, skpo) 10 times. Leave sts on a st-holder ***. Rep from *** to *** to last section. With right side facing, using B k up 10 sts down left-hand side of last section, turn and cont thus: p 2 tog, p 8, turn and k 9; p 2 tog, p 7, turn and k 8; p 2 tog, p 6, turn and k 7; p 2 tog, p 5, turn and k 6; p 2 tog, p 4, turn and k 5; p 2 tog, p 3, turn and k 4; p 2 tog, p 2, turn and k 3; p 2 tog, p 1, turn and k 2; p 2 tog, turn and k 1. Fasten off **.

3rd Band. **** With wrong side facing, using C p up 10 sts down side of last section, turn and work over these and next group of sts on spare needle thus: (k 10, turn and p 9, p 2 tog) 10 times. Leave sts on a spare needle ****. Rep from **** to **** to end.

4th Band. Now with D rep from ** to ** once.

5th Band. With A rep from **** to **** to end.

6th Band. With B rep from ** to ** once.

7th Band. With C rep from **** to **** to end.

8th Band. With D rep from ** to **.

9th Band. ***** With wrong side facing, using A p up 10 sts down side of next section, turn and k 10. Work over these and next group of sts on spare needle thus: p 2 tog, p 7, p 2 tog, turn and k 9; p 2 tog, p 6, p 2 tog, turn and k 8; p 2 tog, p 5, p 2 tog, turn and k 7; p 2 tog, p 4, p 2 tog, turn and k 6; p 2 tog, p 3, p 2 tog, turn and k 5; p 2 tog, p 2, p 2 tog, turn and k 4; p 2 tog, p 1, p 2 tog, turn and k 3; (p 2 tog) twice, turn and k 2; p 3 tog turn and k 1; p 2 tog and fasten off *****. Rep from ***** to ***** to end.

SLEEVES: With 5½mm needles and A cast on 30 sts. Work 7 cm k 1, p 1 rib.

Inc row. (K 2, inc in next st) 10 times. (40 sts) Change to 6½mm needles and rep from 1st band to end of band 6. With C rep from ***** to ***** of back and front to end of band.

SHOULDER AND NECKBANDS: With right side facing, using 5½mm needles and A k up 50 sts along top edge of one piece for back or front. Work 5 rows k 1, p 1 rib. Cast off ribwise. Work other piece to match.

MAKING UP: Do not press. Join cast-off edges of shoulder bands for 14 sts at each end. Beg and ending at centre of 2nd B band, sew top of sleeves to sides. Join side and sleeve seams.

BACK and FRONT

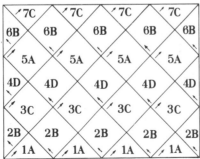

SLEEVES

Arrows: show direction of stocking stitch. Shapes with arrows pointing to the right begin purl or pick up purlwise; shapes with arrows pointing to the left begin knit or pick up knitwise.

Figures: indicate bands. All shapes with the same band number must be completed before the next band is started.

Letters: indicate colours.

Patchwork squares

This glorious combination of vibrant colour and glowing mohair is actually knitted all in one piece with just two seams to join afterwards.

MATERIALS: Argyll Finesse Mohair: 3 (50g) balls each 1st colour cherry (A) and 2nd colour red (B), 2 balls each 3rd colour pink (C), 4th colour wine (D) and 5th colour purple (E); 6½mm (No 3) knitting needles; spare double-pointed needles.

Measurements: To fit 81 to 97 cm, 32 to 38 inch bust very loosely – actual meas, 126 cm; length, 66·5 cm; sleeve, 35 cm.

Tension: 18 sts, 36 rows to 15 cm.

Abbreviations: See page 7.

Note. – For 4 or 9 check squares, do not strand yarns but use a separate ball for each block of colour and twist yarns on wrong side when changing colour to avoid holes. Refer to diagram throughout. All shapes arrowed to right in diagram are picked up purlwise with wrong side facing and worked in purl g st (every row p) beg at left-hand edge of diagram; all shapes arrowed to left in diagram are picked up knitwise with right side facing and worked in knit g st (every row k) beg at right-hand edge of diagram. Break off yarn and leave sts on a spare needle when each shape is complete.

MAIN PART: Beg at lower edge of front. With A cast on 54 sts.

Work **base triangles** (arrowed to right) thus: * P 2, turn and p 2; p 3, turn and p 3; p 4, turn and p 4; cont in this way until p 18, turn and p 18 is worked. Leave sts *. Join A to inner end of rem sts and work from * to * twice.

Work **right-hand side triangle** (arrowed to left) thus: With C beg at lower end of last set of sts, k 2, turn and k 2; inc in 1st st, then sl next st, k next st of triangle, psso – referred to as skpo, turn and k 3; inc in 1st st, k 1, skpo, turn and k 4; cont in this way until inc in 1st st, k 15, skpo, turn, k 18 is worked. Leave sts.

Work **plain square** (arrowed to left) with D thus: K up 17 sts down 2nd side of same base triangle, k 1 st of next triangle, ** turn and k 18; k 17, skpo, turn and k 18; cont until all sts of previous shape are worked, ending k 18. Leave sts **. Work next square with B

and k up 17 sts down left-hand side of 2nd base triangle, k 1 from next triangle and work from ** to **.

Work **left-hand side triangle** (arrowed to left) with C thus: K up 18 sts down left-hand side of last edge. Dec 1 st at beg of next and every alt row until all sts are worked off.

Beg at left-hand side and work **4-check square** (arrowed to right) thus: Along side of triangle p up 9 sts D and 8 sts E, p 1 st E from next square, turn. *** With colours as set p 18, turn, (p 17, then sl 1, p next st of last shape, psso – referred to as sppo, turn and p 18) 8 times ***. Change colours thus: P 9 sts E and 8 sts D, sppo D, turn. Rep from *** to ***. Leave sts. Picking up sts from side of squares of previous band and using colours as given in diagram work next 2 squares.

Beg at right and using B work as right-hand side triangle over sts of previous shape. With A work plain square (arrowed to left) along side of 4-check square. Work **9-check square** (arrowed

to left) thus: Down side of next 4-check square k up 6 sts B, 6 sts A and 5 sts C, k 1 st C from next square. With colours as set, k 18, turn, (k 17, skpo, turn and k 18) 5 times. Change colours thus: K 6 sts A, 6 sts C, 5 sts B and skpo B. With colours as set, k 18, turn and rep bracketed inst 5 times. Change colours thus: K 6 sts C, 6 sts B, 5 sts A and skpo A. With colours as set, k 18, turn and rep bracketed inst 5 times. Leave sts.

Cont in this way working side triangle and next band of squares in colours and direction as given in diagram – work plain square (arrowed to right) as 4-check square but in 1 colour and 9-check square (arrowed to right) with 6 sts and 12 rows in each colour.

For lower edge of 1st sleeve cast on 18 sts C and 9 sts A. With A work corner triangle thus: Inc purlwise in 1st st, turn and p 2; inc in 1st st, p 2, turn and p 4; cont in this way until inc in 1st st, p 16, turn and p 18 is worked. Leave sts. With C over rem 18 sts work as base triangle from * to *.

For lower edge of 2nd sleeve cast on 9 sts C and 18 sts A. With A work as base triangle from * to *. Work corner triangle with C as base triangle until p 9, turn and p 9 is worked, then dec 1 st at end of next and every alt row until all sts are worked off.

Cont working bands of squares as given in diagram including sleeve shapes, working 4-check square (arrowed to left) as plain square but changing colour after 9th st and 18th row. Neck

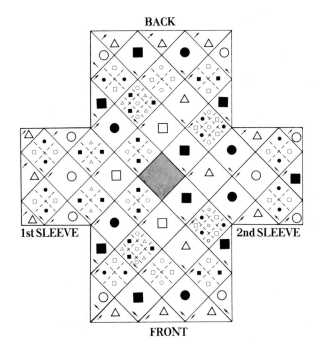

BACK

1st SLEEVE   2nd SLEEVE

FRONT

△ A
■ B
○ C
● D
□ E

opening is shown as toned square in centre of diagram – for neck edges cast off B square on front and cast on 17 sts for opposite 4-check square on back. With A work centre triangle of 1st sleeve edge as given for right-hand side triangle but work p instead of k. With B work centre triangle of 2nd sleeve edge as given for left-hand side triangle but work p instead of k.

For upper edge of 1st sleeve work corner triangle with A as right-hand side triangle working p instead of k until inc in 1st st, p 7, sppo, turn and p 10 is worked. Cont thus: P 2 tog, p 7, sppo, turn and p 9; p 2 tog, p 6, sppo, turn and p 8; cont in this way until all sts are worked off. Work top triangle with C and p up 17 sts across previous shape and p 1, turn and p 18; p 2 tog, p 15, sppo, turn and p 17; cont in this way until all sts are worked off.

For upper edge of 2nd sleeve work top triangle with A as top triangle of 1st sleeve. Work corner triangle with C thus: P up 18 sts, turn and p 18. Dec 1 st each end of next and every alt row until all sts are worked off. Cont working back from diagram, working last 3 triangles at edge of back with A as top triangle of sleeves.

NECK EDGING: With A k up 18 sts across each square of front neck. K 6 rows. Cast off. Work back neck to match.

CUFFS: With A k up 36 sts across end of sleeve. K 6 rows. Cast off.

WELTS: With A k up 54 sts across lower edge of front. K 6 rows. Cast off. Work back welt to match.

MAKING UP: Join side and sleeve seams. Join ends of neck edging.

Aran blocks

The stitches aren't difficult, the technique for interlocking the blocks of knitting is fascinating to do – and the result? It's absolutely amazing!

MATERIALS: 29 (50g) balls Emu Aran; 4mm (No 8) and 5mm (No 6) knitting needles; 4mm (No 8) circular knitting needle, 80 cm long for collar; cable needle; 3 long circular knitting needles, 5mm (No 6) or finer for use as stitch-holders.

Measurements: To fit up to 112 cm, 44 inch bust very loosely – actual meas, 132 cm; length, 74 cm; sleeve, 51 cm.

Tension: 33 sts to 14 cm; 24 rows to 8·5 cm. Equivalent to 10 sts and 12 rows to 5 cm worked in stocking stitch.

Note. – Main part of front, back and sleeves is worked in one piece with welts, cuffs and collar added. If you'd like a smaller version of this sweater – actual chest measurement 104 cm, length, 64 cm and sleeve 42 cm, you'll need 18 (50g) balls of Emu Double Knitting and 3¼mm and 4mm knitting needles. Work to a tension equivalent to 11 sts and 15 rows to 5 cm in stocking stitch and just follow the instructions below and you will have a perfectly scaled down sweater.

Abbreviations: See page 7.

MAIN PART: Use 5mm needles throughout and beg above front welt. See pages 40 and 41 for charts.

1st BAND: Cast on 99 sts.

Base Triangle: Reading 1st and all wrong side rows from left to right; 2nd and all right side rows from right to left, work in patt from chart 3 thus: * **1st row** (wrong side). K 2, turn. **2nd row.** P 2. **3rd row.** K 3, turn. **4th row.** P 3. While working 1 st more before turning on next and every alt row and 2 sts more on 19th, 21st, 23rd, 25th, 39th, 41st and 43rd rows as shown at stepped edge, cont until chart is completed. Break yarn and leave sts on a st-holder **. With wrong side facing, rejoin yarn at

inner end of rem sts and rep from * once more, then rep from * to ** again leaving sts on same st-holder.

2nd BAND: Right-hand Edge Triangle: Cast on 1 st. With right side of work facing, p 1 st from st-holder along side of last shape worked, turn. Reading chart as given for base triangle, cont working patt from chart 3 thus: **1st row** (wrong side). K 2. **2nd row.** P 1, p next st tog with next st from st-holder, turn. **3rd row.** K 1, inc. **4th row.** P 2, p next st tog with next st from st-holder, turn. **5th row.** K 2, inc. **6th row.** P 3, p next st tog with next st from st-holder, turn. **7th row.** K 3, inc. While working last st tog with next st from st-holder at left-hand edge on right side rows *at the same time* inc 1 st on wrong side rows at right-hand edge and inc 2 sts (k into front back and front of st) on 19th, 21st, 23rd, 25th, 39th, 41st and 43rd rows as shown at stepped edge, until chart is completed. Leave sts on 2nd st-holder.

Block Leftwise: * With right side facing, k up 26 sts down adjacent side of shape from which st-holder sts have been worked, p 1st st from next set of sts on st-holder and pass previous st over it, turn. Reading from left to right work inc row of chart 1 (b). Now reading 1st and right side rows from right to left; 2nd and wrong side rows from left to right, work patt from chart 2 thus: **1st row.** Patt 32, p last st tog with next st from st-holder, turn. **2nd row.** Patt 33. Cont in this way and p tog last st of every right side row with 1 st from st-holder until 24th row of chart is completed, rep 1st to 24th rows again and finally work 49th (dec) row. Leave sts on 2nd st-holder. Rep from * again.

Left-hand Edge Triangle: With right side facing, k up 26 sts down adjacent side of last shape from which st-holder sts have been worked. Reading rows as given for chart 3, cont in patt from chart 4 thus: Working right-hand edge straight as chart (no side edge sts to be taken tog) and at left-hand edge, dec 1 st

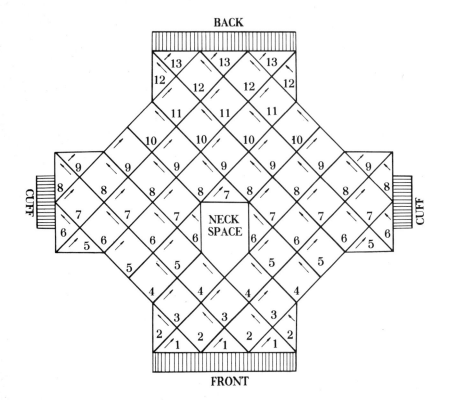

BACK

CUFF

NECK SPACE

CUFF

FRONT

NOTE FOR DIAGRAM

Arrows show direction of cable patts. Shapes with arrows pointing to the right begin purl or pick up purlwise; shapes with arrow pointing to the left begin knit or pick up knitwise.

Figures indicate bands. All shapes with the same band number must be completed before the next band is started.

at beg of 3rd and every alt row and dec 2 sts (k or p 3 tog) at beg of 23rd, 25th, 27th, 29th, 43rd, 45th, and 47th rows as shown by stepped edge, until chart is completed. Fasten off.

3rd BAND: Block Rightwise: * With wrong side facing, p up 26 sts down side of last shape worked, k 1 st from next set of sts on st-holder and pass previous st over it, turn. Reading 1st row from right to left, work inc row of chart 1 (a), then patt 2nd row to last st, s1 1, k 1 st from st-holder, psso, turn. Now cont in patt from chart 2 thus: **1st row.** Patt 33. **2nd row.** Patt 32, s1 1, k 1 st from st-holder, psso, turn. Rep last 2 rows until 24th row of chart is completed, rep 1st to 24th rows again and finally work 49th (dec) row. Leave sts on a st-holder. Rep from * twice more.

4th BAND: 1st Block: Cast on 26 sts, with right side facing, p 1 st from st-holder, pass previous st over it, turn. Work inc row of chart 1 (b), then cont working Block Leftwise as 2nd Band and leave sts on st-holder. Work 2nd block as given for Block Leftwise in 2nd Band but cast off rem sts to form one side of neck V. Work 3rd block as Block Leftwise. For 4th Block k up 26 sts down adjacent side and work straight as chart (no side sts to be taken tog) and leave rem sts on st-holder. K up 26 sts down left-hand edge of last block and cast off for side seam edge.

5th BAND: * Cast on 33 sts and work a Base Triangle as given in 1st Band. Leave sts on a st-holder *. For 1st Block cast on 26 sts, with wrong side facing, k 1 st from st-holder of last block of 4th band and pass previous st over. Complete as Block Rightwise. Work 1 more block, miss adjacent edge to leave space for neck as shown in diagram, work one block on next edge, then for 4th block p up 26 sts and work straight as charts (no side sts to take tog) and leave sts on st-holder. K up 26 sts down right-hand edge of last block and cast off for side seam edge. Work from * to * again.

6th BAND: * Make right-hand edge triangle as given in 2nd band. Make 2 Blocks Leftwise, then make Left-hand Edge Triangle *. Leave space for neck and rep from * to * again as diagram.

7th BAND: Make 3 Blocks Rightwise, cast on 33 sts and make a Base Triangle, then make 3 Blocks Rightwise.

8th BAND: Make a Right-hand Edge Triangle, 6 Blocks Leftwise, then a Left-hand Edge Triangle.

9th BAND: Reverse Base Triangle: * With wrong side facing, p up 26 sts along side of previous shape, k 1 st from st-holder and pass previous st over it, turn. Work 2 rows as chart 1 (a), then beg with 2nd row (reading from right to left), cont in patt from chart 4 while dec 1 st at beg of every alt row (single steps) and 2 sts for double steps on chart *at the same time* sl last st of every alt row, k next st from st-holder, psso. Cont until 1 st rem. Fasten off *. Work 5 Blocks Rightwise, casting off rem sts of last of these blocks. Rep from * to * again. K up 26 sts along side of first of these blocks and cast off for side seam edge.

10th BAND: Omit triangles of previous band and between previous blocks work 4 Blocks Leftwise as shown in diagram, casting off rem sts of last of these blocks. K up 26 sts along side edge of 1st of these blocks and cast off for side seam edge.

11th BAND: Work 3 Blocks Rightwise.
12th BAND: As 2nd band.
13th BAND: Make 3 Reverse Base Triangles.

WELTS: With right side facing, using 4mm needles, k up 98 sts across straight edge of front. Work 22 rows k 2, p 2 rib. Cast off ribwise. Work back welt to match.

CUFFS: With right side facing, using 4mm needles k up 66 sts across straight end of sleeve. **1st row.** K 2, p 2, (k 2 tog, k 1, p 2 tog, p 1) 10 times, k 2. (46 sts) Beg 1st row p 2, work 17 rows k 2, p 2 rib. Cast off ribwise.

COLLAR: With right side facing, using 4mm circular needle, beg at point of V at centre front and k up 26 sts across side of block, 41 sts across side of triangle, 38 sts across base triangle at back, 41 sts across side of triangle, 26 sts across side of block, ending at point of V. (172 sts) Work forward and back in rows. **1st row.** K 1, (p 2, k 2) to last 3 sts, p 2, k 1. **2nd row.** K 3, (p 2, k 2) to last st, k 1. Rep these 2 rows 18 times more, then 1st row again. Cast off loosely ribwise.

MAKING UP: Press work lightly. Join sleeve and side seams, including cuffs and welts. Overlap ends of neckband at V and sew down ends across picked up sides of blocks. Press seams.

Chart 2

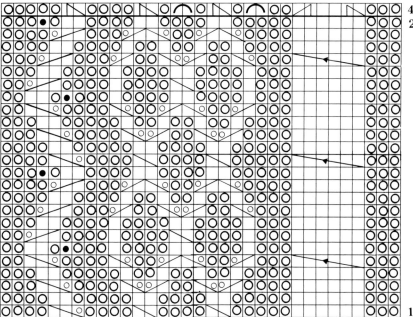

49
24

Begin here ▲

1

Chart 1 (b)

▲ **Begin here**

Chart 1 (a)

Begin here ▲

Chart 3 (for base triangles and right-hand edge triangles)

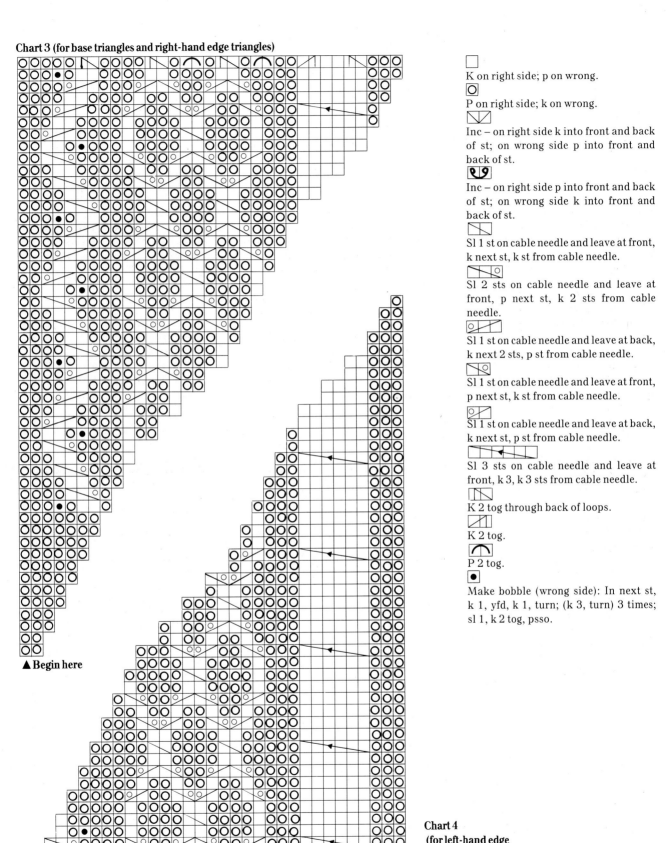

▲ Begin here

▲ Begin here

Chart 4
(for left-hand edge
triangles and reverse
base triangles)

☐
K on right side; p on wrong.

Ⓞ
P on right side; k on wrong.

Inc – on right side k into front and back of st; on wrong side p into front and back of st.

Inc – on right side p into front and back of st; on wrong side k into front and back of st.

Sl 1 st on cable needle and leave at front, k next st, k st from cable needle.

Sl 2 sts on cable needle and leave at front, p next st, k 2 sts from cable needle.

Sl 1 st on cable needle and leave at back, k next 2 sts, p st from cable needle.

Sl 1 st on cable needle and leave at front, p next st, k st from cable needle.

Sl 1 st on cable needle and leave at back, k next st, p st from cable needle.

Sl 3 sts on cable needle and leave at front, k 3, k 3 sts from cable needle.

K 2 tog through back of loops.

K 2 tog.

P 2 tog.

●
Make bobble (wrong side): In next st, k 1, yfd, k 1, turn; (k 3, turn) 3 times; sl 1, k 2 tog, psso.

Painting by knitting

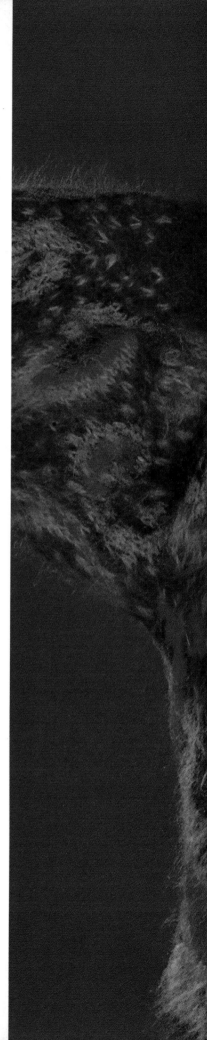

ou've a sense of humour – even when you're knitting? You'd like to paint – but you *knit* instead? Then this collection of favourite pictures and rich motifs has the perfect sweater for you. And if you've never knitted with more than one colour before? Well, take your courage in your hands and look carefully at the instructions. We tell you exactly how to handle the yarns for your chosen sweater. After all, if you can knit stocking stitch, you can tackle these!

PAISLEY

Picture postcard

Knit a bit of good, clean fun with this jolly, motif sweater.

MATERIALS: Jamieson & Smith's 2 ply Jumper Weight Shetland Wool – 4 ply equivalent (see suppliers' list for address and telephone number on page 126): 5 oz green 92 (A), 3 oz sky 75 (B) and 1 oz each red 93 (C), yellow 91 (D), pale pink 101 (E), pink 95 (F), rust 125 (G), orange 73 (H), white 1 (I), black 77 (J), jade 71 (K); 2¾mm (No 12) and 3¼mm (No 10) knitting needles.

Measurements: To fit 81 to 91 cm, 32 to 36 inch bust – actual meas, 104 cm; length, 54 cm; sleeve, 46 cm.

Tension: 16 sts to 6 cm; 18 rows to 5 cm.

Abbreviations: See page 7.

Note. – See pages 46, 47 and 48 for charts. The first 31 rows of s st on back, 27 rows on front and 108 rows on sleeves are shown on charts because the individual sts of I and K are Swiss Darned over these areas afterwards. Ignore single curved lines and dots (eg for crab claws and other features) while working from charts as these indicate lines to be embroidered.

When working motifs, use a separate ball of yarn for each block of colour, twisting yarns together on wrong side when changing colour to avoid holes. In small areas of repeating colour within motif, strand yarn not in use loosely across wrong side to avoid puckering.

BACK: With 2¾mm needles and A cast on 140 sts. Work 28 rows k 1, p 1 rib. Change to 3¼mm needles *. Beg k, work 31 rows s st. Cont in s st and work from 32nd row of chart 1, reading next and all wrong side rows from left to right and all right side rows from right to left. Cont until 118th row of chart is completed. Cont with B; work 52 rows.

Shoulder Shaping: Cast off 54 sts at beg of next 2 rows. Leave 32 sts.

FRONT: As back to *. Beg k, work 27 rows s st. Cont in s st and work from 28th row of chart 2 in the same way as chart 1. Cont until 116th row of chart is completed. Cont with B only and work 20 rows.

Neck Shaping: Next row. K 62 sts, turn. Cont on these sts only. Dec 1 st at neck edge on next 8 rows. Work 25 rows straight. Cast off rem 56 sts. Slip centre 16 sts on a st-holder. Rejoin yarn and k to end. Complete as first side, reversing neck shaping.

SLEEVES: With 2¾mm needles and A cast on 67 sts. Work as back to *. Beg k, cont in s st and inc 1 st each end of 5th and every foll 4th row until there are 113 sts. Work 15 rows, then work last 3 rows of chart 3. Cont with B and work 29 rows. Cast off loosely.

EMBROIDERY: Press work. Still working from all 3 charts, Swiss Darn waves over individual sts in I and K as shown. Working from single curved lines indicated on charts, Back Stitch outlines of features thus: Man's jawline and ear, division of arms and legs and woman's nose with H, his nose and centre of ear with G, mouths with C, eyes, eyebrows and hair with J.

With straight stitches fill in mouths and embroider hair, crab's claws and eyes with J. Fill in eyes with I and J. Work spots on her headscarf with I.

NECKBAND: Join right shoulder. With right side facing, using 2¾mm needles and B, k up 28 sts down left side of front neck, k 16 centre front sts, k up 28 sts up right side of neck and k back neck sts. (104 sts) Work 4 rows k 1, p 1 rib. Cast off ribwise.

MAKING UP: Join left shoulder and neckband seam. Beg and ending 21 cm from shoulders, sew cast-off edge of sleeves to sides. Join side and sleeve seams. Press seams.

Chart
1 ☒ I ☉ K

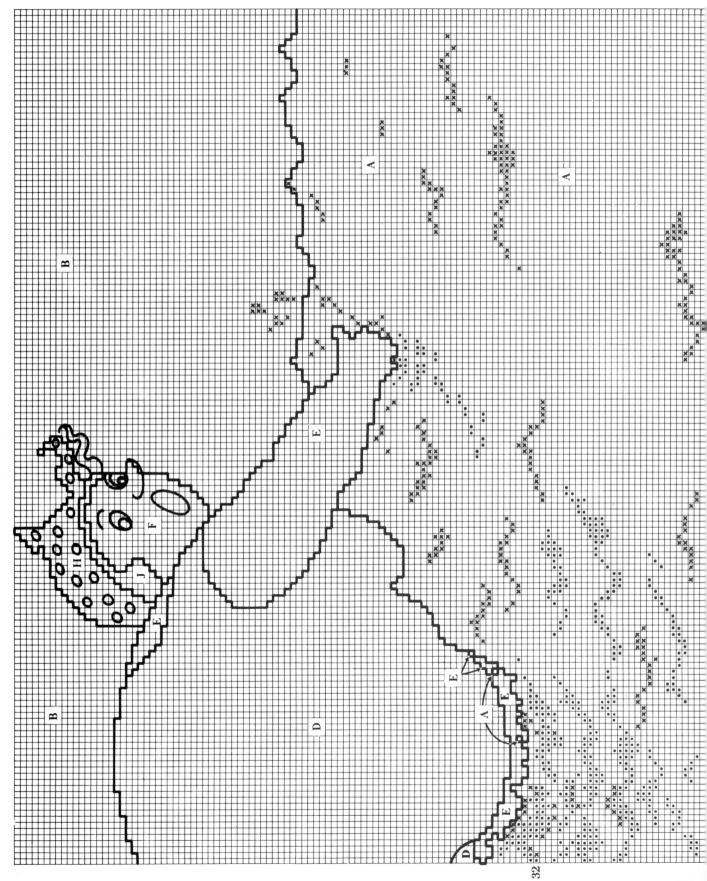

Chart
2 ☒ I ● K

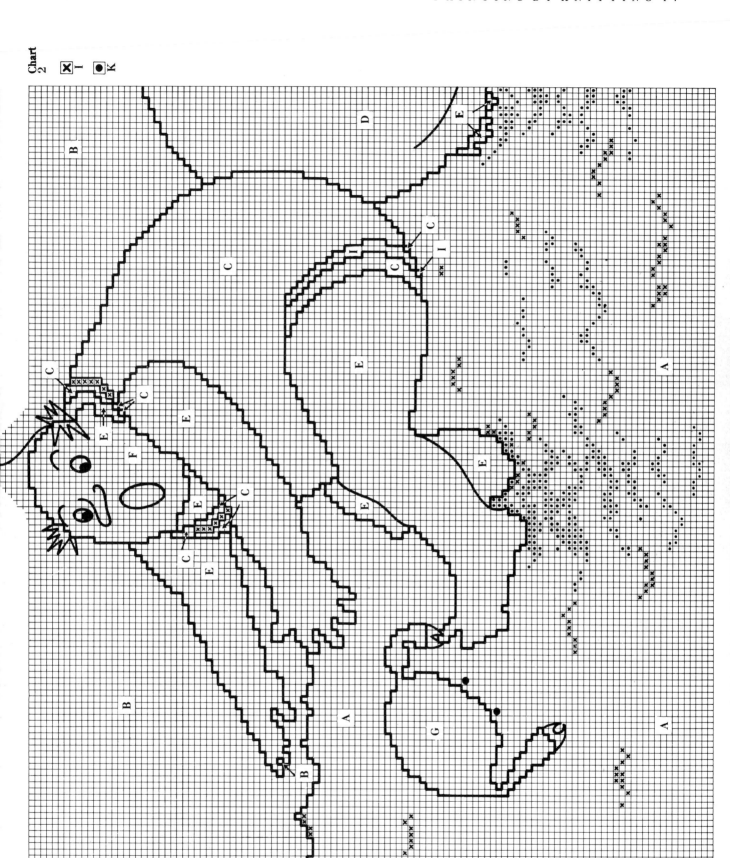

Chart
3 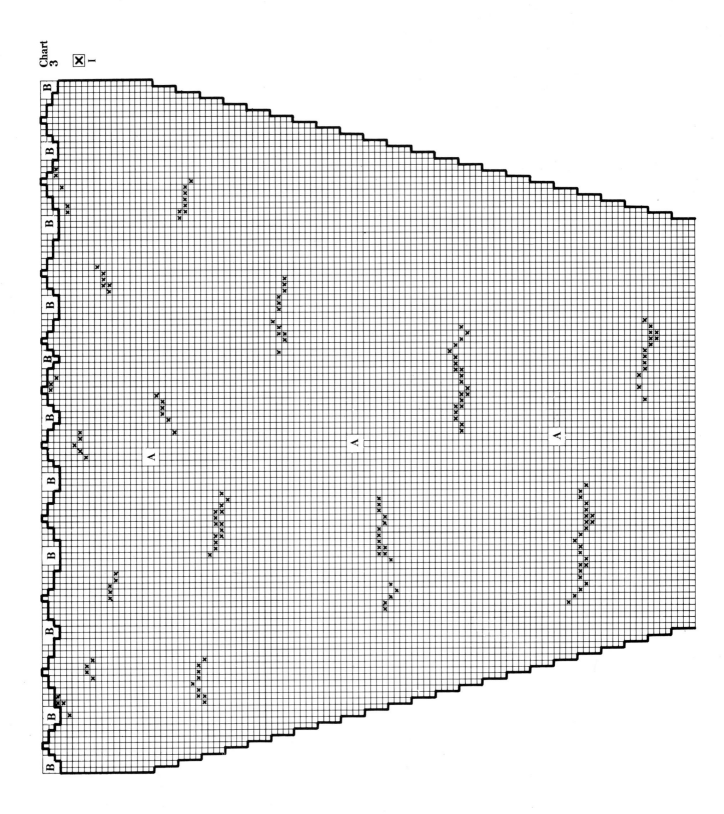 — I

Jum-purr

Look on the light side with this adorable cartoon cat sweater in soft mohair.

MATERIALS: Sirdar Nocturne: 6 (7:7:8) 50g balls main colour pink (A), 1 ball each 2nd colour grey (B), 3rd colour black (C) and 4th colour white (D); 4mm (No 8) and 5½mm (No 5) knitting needles.

Measurements: To fit 81 (86:91:97) cm, 32 (34:36:38) inch bust – actual meas, 94 (99:104:109) cm; length, 62 (62:63:63) cm; sleeve, 42 cm.

Tension: 16 sts, 21 rows to 10 cm.

Abbreviations: See page 7.

Note. – When working motif, use a separate ball of yarn for each block of colour, twisting yarns together on wrong side when changing colour to avoid holes.

BACK: With 4mm needles and A cast on 69 (73:77:81) sts. Work 7 cm k 1, p 1 rib. **Inc row.** Rib 6 (8:10:12), inc, (rib 7, inc) 7 times, rib 6 (8:10:12). 77 (81:85:89) sts. Change to 5½mm needles *. Beg k, cont in s st until work meas 40 cm, ending p.

Armhole Shaping: Cast off 6 sts at beg of next 2 rows. Cont straight until work meas 62 (62:63:63) cm, ending p.

Shoulder Shaping: Cast off 10 (11:12:13) sts at beg of next 2 rows and 11 (12:12:13) sts at beg of foll 2 rows. Leave 23 (23:25:25) sts on a st-holder.

FRONT: As back to *. Beg k, work 14 rows s st. Cont in s st working motif from chart, ignoring lettering within dotted line, thus: **1st row.** K 9 (11: 13:15) A, reading from right to left k 60 sts of 1st row of chart, k 8 (10: 12:14) A. **2nd row.** P 8 (10:12:14) A, reading from left to right p 60 sts of 2nd row of chart, p 9 (11:13:15) A. Cont working patt from chart as set until 56th row of chart is completed.

Armhole Shaping: Cont in patt, casting off 6 sts at beg of next 2 rows. Patt straight until chart is completed. Cont with A. Work 9 (9:11:11) rows.

Neck Shaping: Next row. K 27 (29: 30:32) sts, turn. Cont on these sts only. Dec 1 st at neck edge on next 6 rows. Work 3 rows straight.

Shoulder Shaping: Cast off 10 (11:12:13) sts at beg of next row. Work 1 row. Cast off 11 (12:12:13) sts.

Sl centre 11 (11:13:13) sts on a st-holder and work other side to match.

SLEEVES: With 4mm needles and A cast on 37 (37:39:39) sts. Work 6 cm k 1, p 1 rib. **Inc row.** Rib 2 (2:4:4), * inc, rib 6 (6:4:4); rep from * to end. 42 (42:46:46) sts. Change to 5½mm needles. Beg k, cont in s st, inc 1 st each end of 3rd and every foll 6th row until there are 68 (68:72:72) sts. Cont straight until work meas 46 cm from beg, ending p. Cast off loosely.

NECKBAND: Join right shoulder. With right side facing, using 4mm needles and A k up 14 sts down left side of front, k 11 (11:13:13) sts from st-holder, k up 14 sts up right side of front, k back neck sts. 62 (62:66:66) sts. Work 6 cm k 1, p 1 rib. Cast off ribwise.

MAKING UP: Join left shoulder and neckband seam. Fold neckband in half to wrong side; catch stitch. Setting 4 cm at side of sleeves to cast-off armhole edges, set in sleeves. Join side and sleeve seams. *Embroidery.* – With contrast thread tack dotted line on front between sts and rows as shown; with C embroider letters inside this area in Back Stitch. Remove tacking. With C Back Stitch 3 whiskers on each side of face and 5 eyelashes on top of head above each eye as shown in picture.

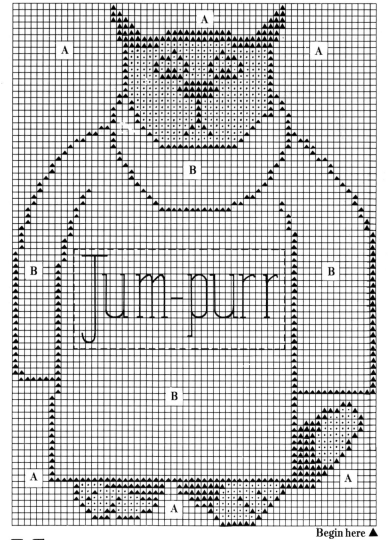

Begin here ▲

C   D

Big cat

This superb sweater, decorated with a fierce, feline face is for tiger lovers everywhere.

MATERIALS: Hayfield Brig DK is no longer available, we suggest using Hayfield Pure Wool Classic Double Knitting: 9 (10:11) 50g balls main colour (A), 1 ball each 2nd colour green (B), 3rd colour black (C), 4th colour white (D) and 5th colour gold (E); 3¼mm (No 10) and 4mm (No 8) knitting needles.

Measurements: To fit 86 (91:97) cm, 34 (36:38) inch bust loosely – actual meas, 104 (109:115) cm; length, 61 (63:64) cm; sleeve, 43 cm.

Tension: 11 sts, 14 rows to 5 cm.

Abbreviations: See page 7.

Note. – When working motif use a separate ball of yarn for each block of colour, twisting yarns together on wrong side when changing colour to avoid holes. In small areas of repeating colour within motif, strand yarn not in use loosely across wrong side to avoid puckering.

FRONT: With 3¼mm needles and A cast on 90 (96:102) sts. Work 7 cm k 1, p 1 rib. **Inc row.** Rib 1 (4:7), pick up loop lying between needles and k into back of it – referred to as m 1, rib 3, m 1, (rib 4, m 1, rib 3, m 1) 12 times, rib 2 (5:8). 116 (122:128) sts. Change to 4mm needles *. Beg k, work 10 rows s st. Cont in s st, working from chart (page 52) thus: **1st row.** K 2 (5:8) A, reading from right to left k 112 sts of 1st row of chart, k 2 (5:8) A. **2nd row.** P 2 (5:8) A, reading from left to right p 112 sts of 2nd row of chart, p 2 (5:8) A. Cont working each row of chart as set until 90th chart row has been worked.

Armhole Shaping: Cast off 6 (7:8) sts at beg of next 2 rows. Dec 1 st each end of next 5 rows. Dec 1 st at beg of next 22 rows, thus completing 119-row chart. 72 (76:80) sts. Cont with A only and work 1 (5:9) rows straight.

Neck Shaping: Next row. K 27 (28:29) sts, turn. Dec 1 st at neck edge on every 3rd row until 20 (21:22) sts rem.

Shoulder Shaping: Cast off 7 sts at beg of next and foll alt row. Work 1 row.

Cast off 6 (7:8) sts. Sl centre 18 (20:22) sts on a st-holder. Rejoin yarn at inner end of rem sts and complete other side of neck to match, reversing shapings.

BACK: As front to *. Beg k, work 100 rows s st.

Armhole Shaping: As front. Work 23 (27:31) rows straight.

Shoulder Shaping: Cast off 7 sts at beg of next 4 rows and 6 (7:8) sts at beg of next 2 rows. Leave 32 (34:36) sts on a st-holder.

SLEEVES: With 3¼mm needles and A cast on 42 (44:46) sts. Work 7 cm k 1, p 1 rib. **Inc row.** Rib 2 (3:4), m 1, (rib 13, m 1) 3 times, rib 1 (2:3). 46 (48:50) sts. Change to 4mm needles. Cont in s st, inc 1 st at each end of every 5th (4th:

4th) row until there are 78 (82:86) sts. Cont until work meas 43 cm. To shape top cast off 6 (7:8) sts at beg of next 2 rows. Dec 1 st each end of next 5 rows. Now cont dec 1 st at beg of every row until 24 sts rem, then cast off 3 sts at beg of next 8 rows.

NECKBAND: Join right shoulder. With right side facing, using 3¼mm needles and A k up 22 sts down left side of neck, k centre front sts, k up 22 sts up right side of neck and k back neck sts. 94 (98:102) sts. Work 6 rows k 1, p 1 rib. Cast off loosely ribwise.

MAKING UP: Press work. Join left shoulder and neckband seam. Set in sleeves. Join side and sleeve seams. Press seams.

Begin here ▲

A B C D E

BIG CAT

Bouquet

Motif-knit a huge posy of flowers on to a simple sweater. Swiss Darn highlights afterwards.

MATERIALS: Rowan Lightweight Double Knitting Wool: 18 (19) 25g hanks green 416 (A), 1 hank each pale green 75 (B), red 42 (C), yellow 13 (D), pink 19 (E), fuchsia 96 (F), clover 128 (G), mauve 121 (H), grey 60 (J), deep pink 41 (K), turquoise 123 (L), crimson 46 (M), brick 45 (N), dark green 73 (P), purple 126 (R), pale pink 20 (S), aubergine 70 (T), orange 17 (U), tan 618 (W) and melon 15 (Z); 3¼mm' (No 10) and 4mm (No 8) knitting needles.

Measurements: To fit 81 to 86 (91 to 97) cm, 32 to 34 (36 to 38) inch bust – actual meas, 94 (104) cm, length, 52 cm; sleeve, 44 cm.

Tension: 12 sts and 15 rows to 5 cm.

Abbreviations: See page 7.

Note. – See pages 56 and 57 for chart. For the larger areas of colour use a separate ball of yarn for each and twist yarns on wrong side when changing colour to avoid holes. Where groups of single stitches occur, work these in predominant colour and Swiss Darn in given colour when knitting is completed.

BACK: With 3¼mm needles and A cast on 115 (127) sts. Work 15 rows k 1, p 1 rib. Change to 4mm needles *. Beg p (wrong side), work 143 rows s st.

Shoulder Shaping: Cast off 36 (42) sts loosely, k 43 sts for back neck and sl these sts on to a st-holder, cast off rem 36 (42) sts.

FRONT: As back to *. Beg p, work 3 rows s st. Now having read note on multi-coloured knitting, work in s st from chart thus: **1st row.** K 7 (13), reading 1st row of chart from right to left, work 101 sts of chart, k 7 (13). **2nd row.** P 7 (13), reading 2nd row of chart from left to right, work 101 sts of chart, p 7 (13). Cont in this way until 116 rows of chart have been worked, ending with a wrong side row.

Neck Shaping: Next row. K 7 (13), work 41 sts at right of chart, turn. Cont on these sts only. Dec 1 st at neck edge on next 12 rows. Work 11 rows straight. Cast off. Sl centre 19 sts on to a spare needle, rejoin yarn and working sts at left of chart, complete to match other side of neck.

SLEEVES: With 3¼mm needles and A cast on 44 (48) sts. Work 18 rows k 1, p 1 rib. Change to 4mm needles and beg k, cont in s st and inc 1 st each end of every 3rd row until there are 116 (122) sts. Work 10 (7) rows. Cast off.

NECKBAND: Matching sts, join right shoulder. With 3¼mm needles and A k up 17sts down left side of front neck, k centre front sts, k up 17 sts up right side of neck and k sts of back neck. (96 sts) Work 6 rows k 1, p 1 rib. Change to H and rib 1 row; cast off ribwise.

MAKING UP: Finish small areas of colour on front of sweater by Swiss Darning these sts. Press work. Join left shoulder and neckband seam. Beg and ending 24 (25) cm from shoulders, sew sleeves on sides. Join side and sleeve seams. Press seams.

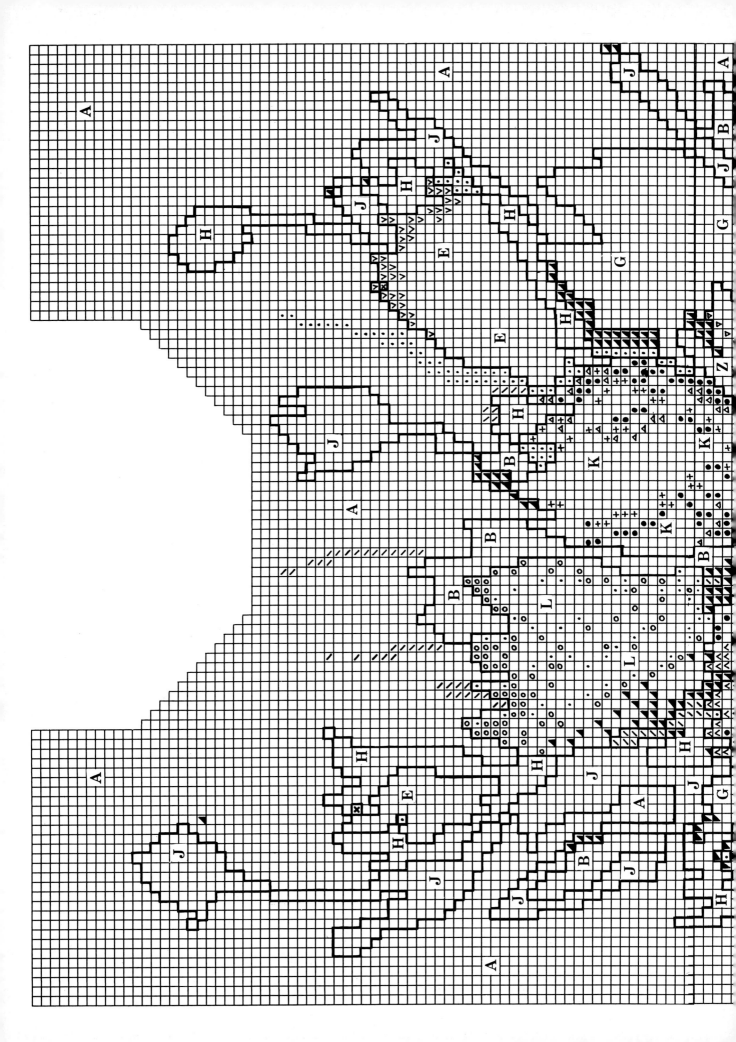

Begin here ▲

⊠ ⊿ ◀ ▶ ⬕ · ↰ ◣ ◁ ▷ ⊡ ⊟ ⊞ ◉
⊠ A B C D E G H J K L M N P R S T U W Z

Paisley

This rich sweater – inspired by the famous patterned shawls – is worked in glowing shades of soft mohair for a sumptuous effect.

MATERIALS: Hayfield Lugano Plain: 4 (50g) balls 1st colour purple (A), 3 balls each 2nd colour gold (B) and 3rd colour blue (C) and 2 balls 4th colour petunia (D); 5mm (No 6) and 6mm (No 4) knitting needles; extra large shoulder pads.

Measurements: To fit 81 to 91 cm, 32 to 36 inch bust – actual meas, 109 cm; length, 51 cm; sleeve, 51 cm.

Tension: 17 sts, 16 rows to 10 cm.

Abbreviations: See page 7.

Note. – While working multi-colour pattern, use separate small balls of yarn for each motif, stranding yarns not in use very loosely across wrong side of work within motif to avoid puckering, twisting them together when changing to background yarn to avoid holes and at the same time stranding yarns for background pattern very loosely across wrong side of entire row, twisting them together when necessary to avoid long strands. Mohair yarns cling together very easily so it is essential to strand loosely and maintain the tension given throughout the work.

BACK: With 5mm needles and B cast on 95 sts. Change to A. K 1 row. Work 9 rows k 1, p 1 rib. Change to 6mm needles. Beg k, cont in s st, working from chart thus *: Reading 1st and all right side rows from right to left, k st before right-hand dotted line, rep 31 sts between dotted lines to last st, k st beyond left-hand dotted line; reading 2nd and all wrong side rows from left to right, p st before left-hand dotted line, rep 31 sts between dotted lines to last st, p st beyond right-hand dotted line. Cont in this way until all 74 rows of chart have been worked.

Shoulder Shaping: Next row. With A, cast off 32 sts, k 31, cast off 32 sts. Leave centre 31 sts on a st-holder for back neck.

FRONT: As back until 66th row of chart has been worked.

Neck Shaping: Cont working in patt from chart. **1st row.** Patt 39 sts, turn. Dec 1 st at neck edge on every row until 32 sts rem. With A cast off. Sl centre 17 sts on to a st-holder, rejoin yarns to inner end of rem sts and work other side to match.

SLEEVES: With 5mm needles and B cast on 33 sts. Work as back to *. Patt as back, inc 1 st each end of 3rd and every foll alt row until there are 95 sts, taking extra sts into patt at each side as they occur. Patt straight until all 74 rows of chart have been worked. With A cast off loosely.

NECKBAND: Join right shoulder seam. With 5mm needles and A k up 10 sts down left side of front, k centre 17 sts, k up 10 sts up right side of front, k 31 back neck sts. Work 9 rows k 1, p 1 rib. With B k 1 row, then cast off loosely knitwise.

MAKING UP: Press very lightly. Join left shoulder and neckband seam. Take 1 st from each edge into seam. Beg and ending 28 cm from shoulder seams, sew cast-off edge of sleeves to sides of back and front. Join side and sleeve seams. Attach shoulder pads.

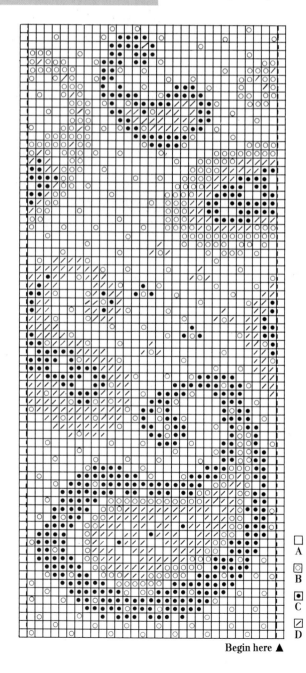

A
☐

B
⊙

C
⦿

D
⊘

Begin here ▲

Abstract jazz

This sweater is easier to make than it looks. The little red triangles are Swiss-Darned at random afterwards.

MATERIALS: Phildar Sagittaire: 6 (7:7:8) 50g balls main colour white (A), 4 (5:5:6) balls 2nd colour black (B) and 1 ball 3rd colour red (C); 3¼mm (No 10) and 4½mm (No 7) knitting needles.

Measurements: To fit 86 (91:97:102) cm, 34 (36:38:40) inch bust – actual meas, 94·5 (102:107:113) cm; length, 53 (54:55:56) cm; sleeve, 44 (45:45: 46) cm.

Tension: 22 sts, 26 rows to 10 cm.

Abbreviations: See page 7.

Note. – When working two-colour knitting, do not weave but strand yarn not in use loosely on wrong side of work to avoid puckering. It is essential to strand loosely and maintain the tension given throughout the work.

BACK: With 3¼mm needles and A cast on 106 (114:120:126) sts. Work 8 rows k 1, p 1 rib. Change to 4½mm needles. Cont in s st, working from chart thus: **1st row.** Beg 1st size at 1, 2nd size at 2, 3rd size at 3 and 4th size at 1 and reading 1st row from right to left k 6 (14:20:6) sts to left-hand edge, rep complete chart 5 (5:5:6) times. **2nd row.** Reading 2nd row from left to right rep complete chart 5 (5:5:6) times,

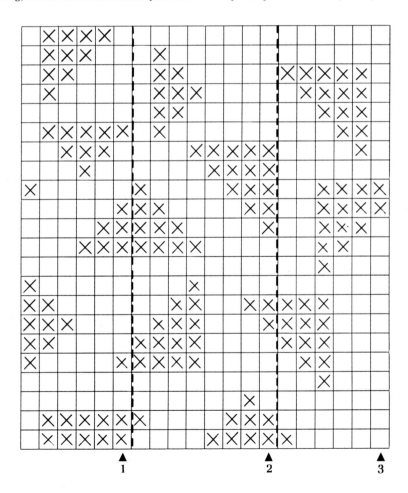

1   2   3

A   B

then work 6 (14:20:6) sts, ending at 1 (2:3:1). Cont working each row of chart in this way. These 22 rows form patt *. Patt until work meas 53 (54:55:56) cm.

Shoulder Shaping: Cast off 15 (17:18:19) sts at beg of next 2 rows and 16 (17:18:19) sts at beg of foll 2 rows. Cast off 44 (46:48:50) sts.

FRONT: As back to *. Patt until work meas 47 (48:49:50) cm, ending p.

Neck Shaping: Next row. Patt 46 (49:51:53), cast off 14 (16:18:20), patt 46 (49:51:53). Cont on last set of sts only. Dec 1 st at neck edge on next 15 rows. Patt 1 row.

Shoulder Shaping: Cast off 15 (17:18:19) sts at beg of next row. Patt 1 row. Cast off. With wrong side facing, rejoin yarns at inner end of rem sts and complete to match other side, reversing shapings.

SLEEVES: With 3¼mm needles and A cast on 60 (60:66:66) sts. Rib 8 rows as back. Change to 4½mm needles. Cont in patt from chart, beg 1st and right side rows of 1st and 2nd sizes at 3 on chart; 3rd and 4th sizes at 1 on chart, then rep complete chart 2 (2:3:3) times *at the same time* inc 1 st each end of 3rd and every foll 4th row until there are 110 (114:118:122) sts, taking these extra sts into patt at each side. Patt 11 (5:9:3) rows straight. To shape top cast off 13 sts at beg of next 8 rows. Cast off loosely.

NECKBAND: Join right shoulder seam. With 3¼mm needles and A k up 66 (68:70:72) sts around front neck and 44 (46:48:50) sts across back neck. Work 21 rows k 1, p 1 rib. Cast off loosely ribwise.

MAKING UP: Press lightly. Join left shoulder and neckband seam. Fold neckband in half to wrong side and catch stitch. Beg and ending 25 (26:27:28) cm from shoulder seams, sew sleeves on sides of back and front. In each 22-row patt rep across back, front and sleeves with C Swiss Darn over 1 or 2 triangles selected at random as shown. Join side and sleeve seams. Press seams lightly.

Flashes of brilliance

Bold dashes and flashing orange spots make a striking sweater in quick-to-knit mohair.

MATERIALS: Tootal Legend Mohair: 8 (50g) balls main colour blue (A), 5 balls 2nd colour black (B) and 1 ball 3rd colour orange (C); 6mm (No 4) and 7mm (No 2) knitting needles.

Measurements: To fit 81 to 97 cm, 32 to 38 inch bust loosely – actual meas, 126 cm; length, 69 cm; sleeve, 43 cm.

Tension: 10 sts to 8 cm; 16 rows to 10 cm.

Abbreviations: See page 7.

Note. – Do not strand yarns, but use a separate small ball for each block of colour, twisting yarns together when changing colour to avoid holes.

BACK: With 6mm needles and A cast on 69 sts. Work 13 rows k 1, p 1 rib. **Inc row.** Rib 7, pick up strand between needles and k it tbl – referred to as m 1, (rib 5, m 1) 11 times, rib 7. (81 sts) Change to 7mm needles. Beg k, cont in s st, working patt from chart thus: **1st row.** Reading 1st row of chart from right to left, using key 1 colours k 27 sts, using key 2 colours k 27 sts, then using key 1 colours k 27 sts. **2nd row.** Reading 2nd row of chart from left to right, using key 1 colours p 27 sts, using key 2 colours p 27 sts, then using key 1 colours p 27 sts. Cont in this way working each row of chart. These 40 rows form patt *. Cont in patt until 20th row of 3rd patt has been worked.

Shoulder Shaping: Next row. With background colours as set, cast off 29, k 23, cast off 29. Leave sts.

FRONT: As back to *. Cont in patt until 40th row of 2nd patt from beg has been worked.

Neck Shaping: Next row. Patt 37, turn. Cont on these sts only. Dec 1 st at neck edge on next 8 rows. Patt 11 rows straight. Cast off loosely. Sl 7 sts at centre on a st-holder, rejoin yarns at inner end of rem sts and work other side to match.

SLEEVES: Using 6mm needles and A cast on 33 sts. Work 11 rows k 1, p 1 rib. **Inc row.** (Rib 3, m 1) 10 times, rib 3. (43 sts) Change to 7mm needles. Beg k, cont in s st working patt from chart thus: **1st row.** Reading 1st row of chart from right to left, beg at * and using key 1 colours k 8 sts, using key 2 colours k 27 sts, using key 1 colours k 8 sts, ending at **. **2nd row.** Reading 2nd row of chart from left to right, beg at ** and using key 1 colours p 8 sts, using key 2 colours p 27 sts, using key 1 colours p 8 sts, ending at *. Cont in patt as set, inc 1 st each end of next and every foll 3rd row, taking extra sts into patt at each side as they occur, until there are 81 sts. Patt 3 rows straight, thus completing 20th row of 2nd patt from beg. Cast off loosely.

NECKBAND: Join right shoulder. With right side facing, using 6mm needles and A k up 19 sts down left side of front, k 7 centre front sts, k up 19 sts up right side of front, k back neck sts. (68 sts) Work 7 rows k 1, p 1 rib. Cast off loosely ribwise.

MAKING UP: Do not press. Join left shoulder and neckband seam. Beg and ending 32 cm from shoulder seams, sew sleeves on sides of back and front. Join side and sleeve seams.

*

** Begin here ▲
** for back and front

KEY 1

A B C

KEY 2

B A C

Bright and breezy

O ut and about, whether it's spring, summer, autumn, winter – wherever you go, whatever you do, there's something here that's just right for you. So choose your style – join the school set, soak up the sun, step out in stripes or navigate a neat nautical twosome. The look that you've been looking for is yours to knit.

Yachting aran

They'll love the cut of your jib in this casual, long sweater with a wide band of diagonal rib across the front. It's just right for breezy days.

MATERIALS: 19 (20:21) 50g balls Patons Diploma for Aran Knitting; 3¾mm (No 9) and 5mm (No 6) knitting needles; cable needle; 4 blazer-type buttons; club badge (optional).

Measurements: To fit 81 (86:91) cm, 32 (34:36) inch bust – actual meas, 95 (100:105) cm; length, 74 (75:76·5) cm; sleeve, 44 cm.

Tension: Over rib patt, 12 sts and 12 rows to 5 cm.

Abbreviations: See page 7.

BACK: With 3¾mm needles cast on 83 (87:91) sts. Beg 1st row k 1, work 19 rows k 1, p 1 rib. **Inc row** (wrong side). P 1, (k 1, p 1, pick up loop lying between needles and k into back of it – referred to as m 1) to last 4 sts, rib 4. 122 (128:134) sts. Change to 5mm needles and patt thus*: **1st row.** P 2, (k 1, p 2) 4 (5:6) times, (k 2, p 3) 13 times, k 2, p 2, (k 1, p 2) 13 (14:15) times. **2nd row.** (K 2, p 1) 13 (14:15) times, k 2, p 2, (k 3, p 2) 13 times, (k 2, p 1) 4 (5:6) times, k 2. **3rd row.** P 2, (k 1, p 2) 4 (5:6) times, (sl next 2 sts on to cable needle and leave at front, p 1, k sts from cable needle – referred to as c 3l, p 2) 13 times, c 3l, p 1, (k 1, p 2) 13 (14:15) times. **4th row.** (K 2, p 1) 13 (14:15) times, k 1, (p 2, k 3) 14 times, (p 1, k 2) 4 (5:6) times. **5th row.** (P 2, k 1) 5 (6:7) times, (c 3l, p 2) 13 times, c 3l, (k 1, p 2) 13 (14:15) times. **6th row.** (K 2, p 1) 13 (14:15) times, (p 2, k 3) 13 times, p 2, k 1, (p 1, k 2) 5 (6:7) times. **7th row.** (P 2, k 1) 5 (6:7) times, p 1, (c 3l, p 2) 14 times, (k 1, p 2) 12 (13:14) times. **8th row.** (K 2, p 1) 12 (13:14) times, k 2, (p 2, k 3) 13 times, p 2, k 2, (p 1, k 2) 5 (6:7) times. **9th row.** P 2, (k 1, p 2) 5 (6:7) times, (c 3l, p 2) 13 times, c 3l,

p 1, (k 1, p 2) 12 (13:14) times. **10th row.** (K 2, p 1) 12 (13:14) times, k 1, (p 2, k 3) 14 times, (p 1, k 2) 5 (6:7) times. **11th row.** (P 2, k 1) 6 (7:8) times, (c 3l, p 2) 13 times, c 3l, (k 1, p 2) 12 (13:14) times. **12th row.** (K 2, p 1) 12 (13:14) times, (p 2, k 3) 13 times, p 2, k 1, (p 1, k 2) 6 (7:8) times. **13th row.** (P 2, k 1) 6 (7:8) times, p 1, (c 3l, p 2) 14 times, (k 1, p 2) 11 (12:13) times. **14th row.** (K 2, p 1) 11 (12:13) times, k 2, (p 2, k 3) 13 times, p 2, k 2, (p 1, k 2) 6 (7:8) times. Patt is now set for centre band of cables moving 1 st to the left on next and foll alt rows. Keeping diagonal band correct after 83rd (89th:95th) row when cables have been worked across all rib sts on left-hand side, still cont until 98th row has been worked.

Armhole Shaping: Cont as set and cast off 11 sts at beg of next 2 rows. Patt 57 (59:63) rows, ending with a right side row. **Dec row.** P 1, (k 2 tog, p 1) to end. 67 (71:75) sts. Change to 3¾mm needles ******. Work 10 rows k 1, p 1 rib. Cast off ribwise.

FRONT: As back to *. **1st row.** P 2, (k 1, p 2) 13 (14:15) times, (k 2, p 3) 13 times, k 2, p 2, (k 1, p 2) 4 (5:6) times. **2nd row.** (K 2, p 1) 4 (5:6) times, k 2, (p 2, k 3) 13 times, p 2, k 2, (p 1, k 2) 13 (14:15) times. **3rd row.** (P 2, k 1) 13 (14:15) times, p 1, (sl next st on to cable needle and leave at back, k 2, p st from cable needle – referred to as c 3r, p 2) 14 times, (k 1, p 2) 4 (5:6) times. **4th row.** (K 2, p 1) 4 (5:6) times, (k 3, p 2) 14 times, k 1, (p 1, k 2) 13 (14:15) times. **5th row.** (P 2, k 1) 13 (14:15) times, (c 3r, p 2) 13 times, c 3r, (k 1, p 2) 5 (6:7) times. **6th row.** (K 2, p 1) 5 (6:7) times, k 1, (p 2, k 3) 13 times, p 2, (p 1,

k 2) 13 (14:15) times. **7th row.** P 2, (k 1, p 2) 12 (13:14) times, (c 3r, p 2) 13 times, c 3r, p 1, (k 1, p 2) 5 (6:7) times. **8th row.** (K 2, p 1) 5 (6:7) times, k 2, (p 2, k 3) 13 times, p 2, k 2, (p 1, k 2) 12 (13:14) times. **9th row.** (P 2, k 1) 12 (13:14) times, p 1, (c 3r, p 2) 14 times, (k 1, p 2) 5 (6:7) times. **10th row.** (K 2, p 1) 5 (6:7) times, (k 3, p 2) 14 times, k 1, (p 1, k 2) 12 (13:14) times. **11th row.** (P 2, k 1) 12 (13:14) times, (c 3r, p 2) 13 times, c 3r, (k 1, p 2) 6 (7:8) times. **12th row.** (K 2, p 1) 6 (7:8) times, k 1, (p 2, k 3) 13 times, p 2, (p 1, k 2) 12 (13:14) times. **13th row.** P 2, (k 1, p 2) 11 (12:13) times, (c 3r, p 2) 13 times, c 3r, p 1, (k 1, p 2) 6 (7:8) times. **14th row.** (K 2, p 1) 6 (7:8) times, k 2, (p 2, k 3) 13 times, p 2, k 2, (p 1, k 2) 11 (12:13) times. Patt is now set for centre band of cables moving 1 st to the right on next and foll alt rows. Keeping diagonal band correct after 83rd (89th : 95th) row when cables have been worked across all rib sts on right hand side, cont as set until 98th patt row has been worked.

Armhole Shaping: Cont as for back from armhole shaping to ******. Work 4 rows k 1, p 1 rib. **Next row** (make buttonholes). Rib 5, cast off 2, rib 6, cast off 2, rib to last 15 sts, cast off 2, rib 6, cast off 2, rib 5. **Next row.** Rib to end casting on 2 sts over those cast off in previous row. Rib 4 more rows. Cast off ribwise.

SLEEVES: With 3¾mm needles cast on 51 (53:57) sts. Rib 15 rows as back. **Inc row** (wrong side). P 1, (k 1, m 1 as given in inc row of back, p 1) to last 4 sts, rib 4. 74 (77:83) sts. Change to 5mm needles and rib patt thus: **1st row.** P 2, (k 1, p 2) to end. **2nd row.** K 2, (p 1, k 2) to end. Cont in rib patt and inc 1 st each end of next and every foll 3rd row until there are 134 (137:143) sts. Work 14 rows straight. Cast off ribwise.

MAKING UP: Press lightly. Lap front shoulder bands over back bands and secure at outer edges. Sew buttons on back band. Sew sleeves into armholes, setting 11 rows of sides of sleeves to cast-off groups at armholes. Join side and sleeve seams. Press seams. Sew badge on right side of front.

Nautical navy

Whatever the weather you'll enjoy being beside the seaside in this long ribbed jacket with tabbed side details.

MATERIALS: 23 (24:25) 50g balls Patons Diploma for Aran Knitting; 3¾mm (No 9) and 5mm (No 6) knitting needles; 9 blazer-type buttons; club badge (optional).

Measurements: To fit 81 to 86 (91 to 97:102 to 107) cm, 32 to 34 (36 to 38:40 to 42) inch bust – actual meas, 111 (116:121) cm; length, 74 cm; sleeve, 44 cm.

Tension: Over rib patt, 14 sts and 28 rows to 8 cm.

Abbreviations: See page 7.

BACK: With 3¾mm needles cast on 101 (105:111) sts. Beg 1st row k 1, work 33 rows k 1, p 1 rib. Change to 5mm needles and patt thus: **1st row** (wrong side). K. **2nd row.** K 1, (p 1, k next st 1 row below st on needle slipping st above off needle in the usual way) to last 2 sts, p 1, k 1. These 2 rows form rib patt *. Cont in rib patt until work meas 74 cm.

Shoulder Shaping: Cast off 10 sts at beg of next 4 rows and 9 (10:12) sts at beg of next 2 rows. Cast off 43 (45:47) sts for back neck.

Welt Trim (2): With right side facing, using 3¾mm needles k up 21 sts along one side edge of rib at lower edge. Beg 1st row p 1, work 3 rows rib as beg. **Next row** (make buttonholes). Rib 4, cast off 2, rib 9, cast off 2, rib 4. Rib 5 more rows casting on 2 sts over those cast off to complete buttonholes on 1st of these rows. Cast off ribwise.

POCKET LININGS (2): With 5mm needles cast on 21 sts. Work 34 rows s st. Leave sts.

LEFT FRONT: With 3¾mm needles cast on 47 (49:51) sts. Work as back to *. Cont in rib patt until work meas 25 cm, ending with a k row. **Pocket Opening row.** Patt 13 (14:15) sts, sl next 21

sts on to a st-holder, with right side facing k 21 sts of one pocket lining, patt 13 (14:15). Cont until work meas 41 cm from beg, ending k.

Front Shaping: Dec 1 st at end of next row and at same edge on every foll 5th row until 29 (30:31) sts rem. Cont until work meas 74 cm, ending k.

Shoulder Shaping: Cast off 10 sts at beg of next and foll alt row. Work 1 row. Cast off 9 (10:11) sts.

RIGHT FRONT: As left, reversing shapings by working 1 row more before front shaping and ending with right side row before shoulder shaping.

SLEEVES: With 3¾mm needles cast on 47 (51:55) sts. Rib 17 rows as at beg of back. Change to 5mm needles and cont in rib patt as back, inc 1 st each end of 3rd and every foll 6th row until there are 91 (95:99) sts. Patt 7 rows. Cast off loosely.

FRONT BAND: Join shoulders. With 3¾mm needles cast on 9 sts. **1st row** (right side). K 2, (p 1, k 1) to last st, k 1. **2nd row.** K 1, (p 1, k 1) to end. Rep last 2 rows once. **Next row** (make buttonhole). Rib 4, cast off 2, rib 3. **Next row.** Rib 3, cast on 2, rib 4. Rib 24 rows, then rep 2 buttonhole rows. Rep last 26 rows 3 times more. Cont in rib until band fits up both fronts and across back neck. Cast off ribwise.

POCKET TOPS (2): Sl sts of one pocket on to 3¾mm needles. Rib 6 rows as set. Cast off ribwise.

MAKING UP: Press lightly. Beg and ending 26 (27:28) cm from shoulder seams, sew cast-off edge of sleeves to sides. Omitting rib at lower edge of back and fronts, join side and sleeve seams. Sew on band and buttons. Lap welt trims over fronts and sew on buttons. Sew down pocket linings and sides of pocket tops. Press seams. Sew badge to left front.

Striped suit

Contrast wide and narrow stripes in smoothest stocking stitch when you knit this stylish big cardigan and matching skirt.

MATERIALS: Avocet Albany Wool Alpaca Double Knitting: *Cardigan.* – 8 (9) 50g balls 1st colour magenta (A), 4 (5) balls 2nd colour black (B) and 2 (3) balls 3rd colour grey (C); 7 buttons. *Skirt.* – Longer length, 6 (7) balls 1st colour magenta (A); shorter length, 5 (6) balls 1st colour magenta (A) and for both lengths, 1 ball each 2nd colour black (B) and 3rd colour grey (C); waist length elastic, 18mm wide. 3¼mm (No 10), 3¾mm (No 9) and 4mm (No 8) knitting needles.

Measurements: *Cardigan.* – To fit 86 to 91 (91 to 97) cm, 34 to 36 (36 to 38) inch bust – actual meas, 110 (117) cm; length, 77 (78) cm; sleeve, 46 cm. *Skirt.* – To fit 91 to 97 (97 to 102) cm, 36 to 38 (38 to 40) inch hip very closely – actual meas, 84 (91) cm; longer length, 80 cm; shorter length, 65 cm.

Tension: 24 sts, 30 rows to 10 cm.

Abbreviations: See page 7.

CARDIGAN

BACK: With 3¼mm needles and B cast on 133 (141) sts. Work 8 rows k 1, p 1 rib. Change to 4mm needles. Beg k, cont in s st stripes of 14 rows B, * 22 rows A, 22 rows B *. Rep from * to * twice **. With A work for 24 (25) cm, ending p.

Neck Shaping: Next row. K 57 (60), cast off 19 (21) sts, k 57 (60). Cont on last set of sts only. Cast off 5 sts at beg of foll 2 alt rows. Work 1 row. Cast off for shoulder. Rejoin yarn at inner end of rem sts and work other side to match.

LEFT FRONT: With 3¼mm needles and B cast on 65 (69) sts. As back to **.

Front Shaping: Cont with A only. Dec 1 st at end of next and every foll 4th row until 47 (50) sts rem. Cont straight until work meas 26 (27) cm from top of last B stripe. Cast off.

RIGHT FRONT: As left, reversing shapings.

SLEEVES: With 3¼mm needles and A cast on 55 (57) sts. Work 5 cm k 1, p 1 rib. **Inc row.** Rib 2 (0), * inc, rib 4 (3); rep from * to last 3 (1) sts, inc, rib 2 (0). 66 (72) sts. Change to 4mm needles. Beg k, while working s st stripes of 4 rows C and 4 rows A *at the same time* inc 1 st each end of every foll 3rd row until there are 132 (138) sts. Work 1 row, thus completing 13th C stripe from beg. Cont with B only and inc 1 st each end of next and every foll alt row until there are 154 (160) sts. Work 1 row. Cast off.

FRONT EDGING: Join shoulder seams. With 3¼mm needles and B cast on 10 sts. With B work 16 rows k 1, p 1 rib. **Buttonhole row.** Rib 4, cast off 2, rib 4. **Next row.** Rib 4, cast on 2, rib 4. Rib 4 rows. With A work 16 rows rib, rep 2 buttonhole rows and rib 4 rows. Rep last 44 rows twice more, then first 22 rows again. Cont with A only and rib until band is long enough from top of last B stripe to fit from 1st dec up shaped edge of right front, around back neck and down shaped edge of left front to 1st dec. Cont in rib stripes of (22 rows B, 22 rows A) 3 times, 22 rows B. With B cast off ribwise.

MAKING UP: Press work. Beg and ending at lower edge of top B stripe, sew sleeves on sides of back and front. Matching stripes, sew on front bands. Join side and sleeve seams. Sew on buttons. Press seams.

SKIRT

BACK AND FRONT ALIKE: With 3¾mm needles and A, for longer length cast on 93 (101) sts; for shorter length cast on 97 (105) sts. Work 8 rows k 1, p 1 rib. Change to 4mm needles. Beg k, work 10 rows s st. While working in s st stripes of 1 row C, 2 rows B, 1 row C, 18 rows A *at the same time* inc 1 st each end of 5th and every foll 26th row until there are 103 (111) sts. Work 23 rows for longer length; 31 rows for shorter length, thus ending with 18th row of 7th A stripe from beg for longer length; 18th row of 5th A stripe from beg for shorter length. Dec 1 st each end of next and every foll 8th row until 83 (91) sts rem. Patt 7 rows thus ending with 10th row of 11th A stripe for longer length; 10th row of 9th A stripe for shorter length. Change to 3¾mm needles. With A only work 16 rows k 1, p 1 rib for waistband. Cast off ribwise.

MAKING UP: Press work. Matching stripes, join side seams. Join ends of elastic. Fold waist rib in half to wrong side enclosing elastic and catch stitch.

Autumn leaves

Take to the hills in this gorse yellow sweater. The beautiful leaves are on both front and back.

MATERIALS: 13 (14) 50g balls 3 Suisses Yves St Laurent Super Lana; 3mm (No 11) and 3¾mm (No 9) knitting needles.

Measurements: To fit 81 to 86 (91 to 97) cm, 32 to 34 (36 to 38) inch bust – actual meas, 99 (105) cm; length, 62 cm; sleeve, 48 cm.

Tension: 25 sts to 10 cm; 36 rows to 11 cm.

Abbreviations: See page 7.

BACK: With 3mm needles cast on 126 (134) sts. Work 7 cm k 2, p 2 rib. Change to 3¾mm needles. Cont in patt from charts thus: Ignore toned areas as these only balance charts to allow space for increased stitches (number of sts varies from row to row). **1st row.** Reading all charts from right to left, k 19 (23), p 6, * work 3 sts of 1st row of chart 1, p 6, work 3 sts of 1st row of chart 2, p 6, work 3 sts of 1st row of chart 1 *, p 8, work 18 sts of 1st row of chart 3, p 8, rep from * to * once, p 6, k 19 (23). **2nd row.** Reading all charts from left to right, p 19 (23), k 6, * work 3 sts of 2nd row of chart 1, k 6, work 3 sts of 2nd row of chart 2 , k 6, work 3 sts of 2nd row of chart 1 *, k 8, work 20 sts of 2nd row of chart 3, k 8, rep from * to * once, k 6, p 19 (23). **3rd row.** Working 3rd row of each chart (now 20 sts of chart 3), work in order as 1st row. **4th row.** Working 4th row of each chart, (now 7 sts of chart 1 and 22 sts of chart 3), work in order as 2nd row. **5th row.** Working 5th row of each chart (now 7 sts of chart 1 and 22 sts of chart 3), work in order as 1st row. **6th row.** K 19 (23), k 6, * work 7 sts of 6th row of chart 1, k 6, work 5 sts of 6th row of chart 2, k 6, work 7 sts of 6th row of chart 1 *, k 8, work 20 sts of 6th row of chart 3, k 8, rep from * to * once, k 6, k 19 (23). These 6 rows form ladder patt panels at each end of work. Rep ladder patt, and cont working from charts as set until 12th row from beg has been worked. Chart 1 has now been completed so to rep patt cont thus: **13th row.** Patt, working 1st row of chart 1 and 13th row of charts 2 and 3. Cont in patt as now set until 24th row from beg has been completed. Chart 3 has now been completed and chart 1 for the second time, so to rep patt cont thus:

25th row. Patt, working 1st row of chart 1, 25th row of chart 2 and 1st row of chart 3. Cont in patt as now set until 36th row from beg has been worked. Chart 2 has now been completed and chart 1 for the third time, so to rep patt cont thus: **37th row.** Patt working 1st row of chart 1 and chart 2 and 13th row of chart 3. Patt as set, returning to 1st row of chart as each is completed until 36th row of 3rd chart 2 has been worked.

Armhole Shaping: Cast off 10 sts at beg of next 2 rows **. Patt straight until 36th row of 5th chart 2 patt from beg has been worked.

Shoulder Shaping: Next row. Cast off 32 (36) sts, break yarn, sl 42 sts on a st-holder, cast off 32 (36) sts.

FRONT: As back to **. Patt straight until 36th row of 4th chart 2 patt from beg has been worked.

Neck Shaping: Next row. Patt 41 (45), p 2 tog, turn. Cont on these sts only. Dec 1 st at neck edge on next 10 rows. Cont in patt until 36th row of 5th chart 2 patt

Chart 2

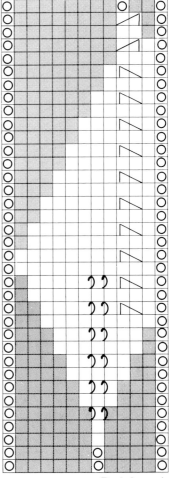

Begin here ▲

Chart 3

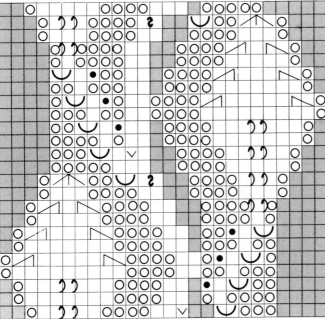

Begin here ▲

from beg has been worked. Cast off. Sl 20 sts at centre on to a st-holder, rejoin yarn and p 2 tog, patt to end. Complete to match other side.

SLEEVES: With 3mm needles cast on 60 sts. Work 7 cm k 2, p 2 rib. **Inc row.** Rib 1, (inc in next st, rib 2) 19 times, inc, rib 1. (80 sts) Change to 3¾mm needles. Beg k, work 5 rows s st. K 1 row. These 6 rows form ladder patt. Cont, inc 1 st each end of next and every foll 6th row until there are 114 sts. Cont until 24th k ridge of ladder patt has been worked. Work 4 rows s st. Cast off.

NECKBAND: Join right shoulder. With 3mm needles k up 35 sts down left side of front, k 20 sts from st-holder, k up 35 sts up right side of front, k 42 back neck sts. (132 sts) Work 3 cm k 2, p 2 rib. Cast off ribwise.

MAKING UP: Press lightly. Join left shoulder. Setting 4 cm at sides of sleeves to cast off sts at armholes, set in sleeves. Join side and sleeve seams.

Ignore toned areas

☐
K on right side; p on wrong.

P on right side; k on wrong.

(K 1, yfd) twice, k 1 all into 1 st.

∨
K into front and back of 1 st.

▣
P into front and back of 1 st.

⌐
Yfd or yrn to make a st.

⊍   ⋈
P 2 tog.   Sl 1, k 1, psso.

◣   ◢
K 2 tog.   Sl 1, k 2 tog, psso.

⌇
Pick up strand lying between needles and k it tbl to make a st.

Chart 1

Begin here ▲

Winter thistle

Keep out the cold in a richly textured sweater. The unusual motif uses simple Aran stitches to create a realistic thistle.

MATERIALS: Phildar Pure New Wool Double Knitting is no longer available, we suggest using 14 (15) 50g balls Phildar Sagittaire; 3¼mm needles (No 10) and 4mm (No 8) knitting needles; cable needle.

Measurements: To fit 81 to 86 (86 to 91) cm, 32 to 34 (34 to 36) inch bust – actual meas, 99 (106) cm; length over

Chart 4

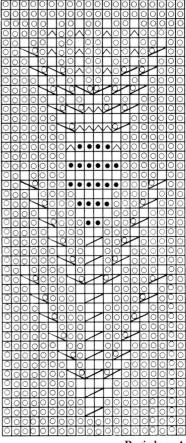

Begin here ▲

m st of side panels, 52 cm; sleeve, 45 cm.
Tension: 9 sts to 4 cm and 24 rows to 7 cm over m st.
Abbreviations: See page 7.
BACK: With 3¼mm needles cast on 118 (126) sts. Work 23 rows k 1, p 1 rib.
Inc row. Rib 5 (4), * pick up loop lying between needles and k into back of it – referred to as m 1, rib 3, m 1, rib 2; rep from * to last 3 (2) sts, rib 3 (2). 162 (174) sts. Change to 4mm needles. Now reading 1st and right side rows of charts from right to left, 2nd and wrong side rows from left to right, patt from charts thus: **1st row** (right side). K 1, (p 1, k 1) 11 (14) times, * p 2, work 6 sts of 1st row of chart 1, p 2, 24 sts of 1st row of chart 2, p 2, 12 sts of 1st row of chart 3 *, 20 sts of 1st row of chart 4, ** 12 sts of 1st row of chart 3, p 2, 24 sts of 1st row of chart 2, p 2, 6 sts of 1st row of chart 1, p 2 **, k 1, (p 1, k 1) 11 (14) times. **2nd row.** Working 2nd row of each chart k 1, (p 1, k1) 11 (14) times, k 2, work 6 sts of chart 1, k 2, 24 sts of chart 2, k 2, 12 sts of chart 3, 20 sts of chart 4, 12 sts of chart 3, k 2, 24 sts of chart 2, k 2, 6 sts of chart 1, k 2, k 1, (p 1, k 1) 11 (14) times.

These 2 rows form m st for 23 (29) sts at each end. Cont until 12th rows of charts have been worked. **13th row.** M st 23 (29), rep from * to * of 1st row, work 20 sts of 13th row of chart 4, rep from ** to ** of 1st row, m st 23 (29). Cont as set, repeating 12 rows of charts 1, 2 and 3 and still work from chart 4 at centre until 46th row of chart 4 has been worked, then beg from 1st row of chart 4 again and cont until 30th row is completed.
Armhole Shaping: Cast off 14 sts at beg of next 2 rows ***. Cont until 18th row of 4th chart 4 patt is completed.
Shoulder Shaping: Cast off 37 (43) sts at beg of next 2 rows. Leave 60 sts.
FRONT: As back to ***. Cont until 46th row of 3rd chart 4 patt is completed.
Neck Shaping: Next row. Patt 50 (56) sts, k 2 tog, turn. Cont on these sts only. Dec 1 st at neck edge on next 14 rows. Work 3 rows. Cast off. Sl centre 30 sts on to a st-holder and complete other side of neck to match.
SLEEVES: With 3¼mm needles cast on 65 sts. Work 37 rows k 1, p 1 rib. **Inc row.** Rib 13, (m 1 as given in inc row of back, rib 2) to last 10 sts, rib 10. (86 sts)

Change to 4mm needles and working from charts as for back, patt thus: **1st row** (right side). K 1, (p 1, k 1) 9 times, p 2, work 12 sts of 1st row of chart 3, 20 sts of chart 4, 12 sts of chart 3, p 2, k 1, (p 1, k 1) 9 times. Cont with centre panel of chart 4 with panels of chart 3 at each side and 19 sts in m st at each end and work 3 rows. Now working inc sts at each end in m st, inc 1 st each end of next and every foll 4th row until there are 130 sts. Cont straight until 46th row of 3rd chart 4 patt is completed. Cast off loosely.
NECKBAND: Join right shoulder. With right side facing, using 3¼mm needles k up 18 sts down left side of neck, k 30 centre front sts, k up 18 sts up right side of neck and k 60 sts of back neck. (126 sts) Work 17 rows k 1, p 1 rib. Cast off loosely.
MAKING UP: Press lightly avoiding bobbles of chart 4. Join left shoulder and neckband seam. Fold neckband in half to wrong side and catch stitch. Sew sleeves into armholes, setting 6 cm of sides of sleeves to cast-off groups of underarms. Join side and sleeve seams.

Chart 3

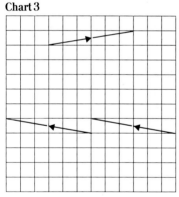

Begin here ▲

Chart 2

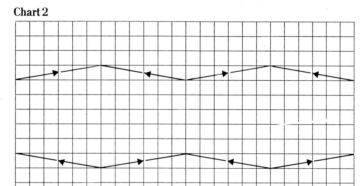

Begin here ▲

Chart 1

Begin here ▲

□
K on right side, p on wrong.

⊙
P on right side, k on wrong.

Sl 3 sts on to cable needle and leave at back, k 3, k sts from cable needle.

Sl 3 sts on to cable needle and leave at front, k 3, k sts from cable needle.

⋀
K 1 tb1.

▱
Take point of right-hand needle in front of 1st st and k 2nd st, k 1st st and sl both sts off needle in the usual way.

▱
Take point of right-hand needle in front of 1st st and k 2nd st, p 1st st and sl both sts off needle in the usual way.

◣◨
Take point of right-hand needle to back of 1st st and p 2nd st, k 1st st and sl both sts off needle in the usual way.

●
K into front, then back and front again of 1 st, turn and p 3, turn and k 3 and pass 2nd and 3rd sts over 1st st and off needle.

Smart blazer

Create that crisp uniform effect with this striped blazer. The body is worked in one – there are no side seams.

MATERIALS: Sunbeam Aran Knit: 15 (50g) balls main colour black (A), 4 balls 2nd colour gold (B) and 2 balls 3rd colour grey (C); 4½mm (No 7) and 5mm (No 6) long knitting needles or circular knitting needles; 4 black buttons; shoulder pads.

Measurements: To fit 81 to 97 cm, 32 to 38 inch bust – actual meas, 112 cm; length, 68 cm; sleeve, 42 cm.

Tension: 17 sts, 23 rows to 10 cm.

Abbreviations: See page 7.

Note. – Direction of knitting lies horizontally across main part and sleeves. If circular needles are used work forward and back in rows. When working front bands with 2 colours, twist yarns together on wrong side when changing colour to avoid holes.

MAIN PART: Beg at left front edge. With 4½mm needles and B by thumb method cast on 100 sts. Beg 1st row k 1, work 2 rows k 1, p 1 rib. **Next row.** With B k 1, p 1, k 1, with A rib to end. **Next row.** With A rib to last 3 sts, with B rib 3. Rep last 2 rows once more. **Next row** (right side). With B cast off 3, with A cast off 2, rib to end. (95 sts) Change to 5mm needles. For lapel with A only cont thus: **1st row.** Rib 43, p 52. **2nd row.** K 54, rib 41. **3rd row.** Rib 39, p 56. Cont in this way working 2 sts more in s st and 2 sts less in rib on every row until row reading rib 31, p 64 has been worked. **8th row.** K 68, rib 27. **9th row.** Rib 23, p 72. Cont in this way working 4 sts less in rib and 4 sts more in s st on every row until row reading k 92, rib 3 has been worked. **Next row.** Cast on 3 sts, p to end. With B k 1 row. **Next row.** With C cast on 14 sts, p to end. K 1 row C; p 1

row B. Cont in s st and work stripes of 14 rows A, 1 row B, 2 rows C, 1 row B. These 18 rows form stripe patt. Cont in patt and work a further 9 rows.

Left Armhole Shaping: * Cast off 32 sts at beg of next row, 7 sts at beg of next alt row, then 3 sts at beg of foll 2 alt rows. Patt 19 rows straight. Cast on 3 sts at beg of next and foll alt row, 7 sts at beg of next alt row and 32 sts at beg of foll alt row, ending with 6th row of A stripe *. For back patt 93 rows straight, ending with 9th row of A stripe.

Right Armhole Shaping: As left from * to *. For right front patt 29 rows straight, ending with C stripe. Cast off 14 sts at beg of next row and 3 sts at beg of foll alt row. For lapel with A only cont thus: **Next row.** K 92, k 1, p 1, k 1. **Next row.** Rib 7, p 88. **Next row.** K 84, rib 11. Cont in this way working 4 sts more in rib and 4 sts less in s st on every row until row reading rib 31, p 64 has been worked. Now work 2 sts more in rib and 2 sts less in s st on every row until row reading rib 43, p 52 has been worked. Change to 4½mm needles. **Next row.** Using 2 needle method of casting on, with A cast on 2, with B cast on 3, then over these sts with B k 1, p 1, k 1, with A rib all sts. **Next row.** With A rib to last 3 sts, with B rib 3. **Buttonhole row.** With B rib 3, with A cast off 2, (rib 13, cast off 2) 3 times, rib to end. **Next row.** With A and casting on 2 sts over those cast off on previous row, rib to last 3 sts, with B rib 3. With B rib 3 rows. Cast off ribwise for right front edge.

Lower Edge: With right side facing using 4½mm needles and A, beg and ending within front rib 5-st cast-on and cast-off edges, k up 165 sts evenly across lower edge of main part. Beg 1st row k 1, work 2 rows k 1, p 1 rib. With B rib 3 rows. Cast off loosely ribwise.

SLEEVES: With 5mm needles and A cast on 8 sts. K 1 row. While casting on

5 sts at beg of next and every alt row for side edge of sleeve *at the same time* work 7 rows A, 1 row B and 1 row C. (33 sts) Cont in stripe patt as main part and while casting on 2 sts at beg of next and foll 6 alt rows for sleeve top *at the same time* still cast on 5 sts at beg of foll 7 alt rows for side. (82 sts) Now shaping sleeve top only, inc 1 st at beg of next and foll 10 alt rows, ending with B stripe. Patt 39 rows straight, ending with B stripe. Dec 1 st at beg of next and foll 10 alt rows. While casting off 5 sts at beg of next and foll 11 alt rows for side, *at the same time* cast off 2 sts at beg of foll 7 alt rows for top shaping. Cast off rem 8 sts.

CUFFS: With right side facing, using 4½mm needles and A k up 49 sts across straight end of sleeve. Complete as lower edge of main part.

COLLAR: Join shoulder seams. With right side facing, using 5mm needles and A and omitting lapel edges, k up 17 sts up right side of front, 31 sts across back neck and 17 sts down left side of front. Beg k 1, work 1 row k 1, p 1 rib. Cont in rib, inc 1 st each end of next and foll 3 alt rows. Rib 10 rows straight. With B rib 3 rows. Cast off very loosely ribwise. Join shaped sides of collar to 8 rows of lapels. Finish rem edges of V between collar and lapel thus: With right side of collar and lapel facing (wrong side of main part), using 4½mm needles and B k up 10 sts along 1 edge, 1 st from seam in V and 10 sts along other edge. **1st row.** (P 1, k 1) 4 times, p 1, sl 1, k 2 tog, psso, p 1, (k 1, p 1) 4 times. Casting off ribwise, k centre 3 sts tog.

LARGE POCKETS (2): With 5mm needles and A cast on 30 sts. Beg 1 row B, 2 rows C, 1 row B, work in stripe patt for 36 rows. Cast off.

Top edging: With right side facing, using 4½mm needles and B, beg left pocket at end of cast-off edge (right pocket at end of cast-on edge) and k up 31 sts across one side of row ends. Rib 3 rows. Cast off ribwise.

BREAST POCKET: Casting on 20 sts work as large pocket for 22 rows.

Top edging: Picking up 19 sts work as edging of left pocket.

MAKING UP: Press work. Join sleeve seams and placing this seam to centre of underarm A stripe, set in sleeves. Join ends of lower edge to front bands. Matching stripes, sew on large pockets just above lower edging; sew on breast pocket with lower edge level with 4th st below underarm. Sew on buttons. Press seams. Sew in shoulder pads.

Squared jacket

This bold jacket, is an easy-to-make cover-up that looks great outdoors.

MATERIALS: Wendy Shetland Chunky is no longer available, we suggest using Wendy Family Choice Chunky: 6 (7) 50g balls 1st colour blue (A), 5 (5) balls 2nd colour gold (B) and 4 (5) balls each 3rd colour red (C), 4th colour royal (D) and 5th colour green (E); 5½mm (No 5) and 6½mm (No 3) knitting needles; 5 toggles.

Measurements: To fit 81 to 91 (97 to 107) cm, 32 to 36 (38 to 42) inch bust loosely – actual meas, 109 (118) cm; length, 68 (69) cm; sleeve, 46 cm.

Tension: 7 sts, 10 rows to 5 cm.

Abbreviations: See page 7.

Note. – Use separate balls of yarn for each block of colour and when changing colour, twist yarns together on wrong side to avoid holes.

BACK: With 5½mm needles and B cast on 78 (84) sts. Beg p, work 10 rows rev s st *. **Hem row** (right side). Fold up hem behind needle and with D (k next st together with corresponding cast on lp) 39 (42) times **, with E rep bracketed inst 39 (42) times. Change to 6½mm needles. **Next row.** P 39 (42) E, 39 (42) D. With colours as set, beg k, work 62 rows s st, then 3 rows rev s st. P 1 row. Break off yarns. **Next row.** K 39 (42) C, 39 (42) B. With colours as now set, beg k, work 3 rows rev s st. Beg k, work 10 rows s st.

Underarm Shaping: Next row. By 2 needle method, cast on 4 sts C and 6 sts E, p 6 E, k 43 (46) C, k B to end. **Next row.** Cast on 4 sts B and 6 sts E, k 6 E, k 4 B, p 39 (42) B, 39 (42) C, k 4 C, k 6 E. Cont with colours as set thus: **1st row.** P 10, k to last 10 sts, p 10. **2nd row.** K 10, p to last 10 sts, k 10. **3rd row.** P 6, k to last 6 sts, p 6. **4th row.** K 6, p to last 6 sts, k 6. **5th row.** As 1st. **6th row.** As 2nd. **7th row.** As 1st. **8th row.** As 4th.

9th row. As 3rd. **10th row.** As 2nd. Rep these 10 rows for ladder st at sides until work meas 25 (26) cm from underarm.

Shoulder Shaping: Cast off 19 (20) sts at beg of next 2 rows and 18 (20) sts at beg of foll 2 rows. Leave 24 sts on a st-holder.

POCKET LININGS (2): Make one D; one E. With 6½mm needles cast on 20 sts. Work 34 rows s st. Leave sts on a st-holder.

RIGHT FRONT: With 5½mm needles and B cast on 39 (42) sts and work as back to *, then with E work hem row to **. Change to 6½mm needles. Cont with E and beg p, work 35 rows s st. **Pocket opening row.** K 10 (11), sl next 20 sts on a st-holder, k 20 sts of E pocket lining, k 9 (11). Work 27 rows s st, then beg p, work 3 rows rev s st. P 1 row. With B k 1 row. Beg k, work 3 rows rev s st, then beg k, work 11 rows s st.

Underarm Shaping: Next row. Cast on 4 sts B and 6 sts D, k 6 D, k 4 B, p B to end. Cont with colours as set. **Next row.** K to last 10 sts, p 10. **Next row.** K 10, p to end. **Next row.** K to last 6 sts, p 6. **Next row.** K 6, p to end. Cont in ladder st patt at side edge as set until work meas 17·5 (18·5) cm from underarm edge, ending with a wrong side row.

Neck Shaping: Cast off 3 sts at beg of next row, then dec 1 st at neck edge on foll 9 rows. Work 5 rows.

Shoulder Shaping: Cast off 19 (20) sts at beg of next row. Work 1 row. Cast off.

LEFT FRONT: As right front, using D instead of E and C instead of B for upper block, reversing pocket opening row and shapings and working ladder st patt as given for right edge of back.

SLEEVES: With 5½mm needles and C cast on 52 (54) sts. Work as back to *, then with A work hem row to ** but rep bracketed inst 52 (54) times. Change to 6½mm needles. Beg p, cont in s st, inc 1 st each end of every 8th row until there are 68 (70) sts. Cont until work meas 43 cm. Cast off.

FRONT BORDERS: With 5½mm needles and A, beg at hem row of right front edge, picking up 1 st from each row, (k up 19 sts, cast on 3 st for buttonhole, miss 4 rows) 5 times, k up 2 (4) sts, ending at neck shaping. Work 6 rows g st. Cast off. Beg at neck edge, k up 112 (114) sts down left front edge, ending at hem row. Work 6 rows g st. Cast off.

COLLAR: Join shoulder seams. With wrong side facing, using 5½mm needles and A, beg and ending at edge of borders, k up 22 sts up left front, k 24 back

sts, k up 22 sts down right front. Beg k, work 3 rows rev s st, then dec 1 st each end of next 15 rows. With E, inc 1 st each end of next 15 rows, then work 2 rows straight. Cast off.

POCKET TOPS: Sl pocket sts on to 5½mm needles. With right side facing, using C k 1 row, then work 7 rows rev s st. Cast off.

MAKING UP: Fold 6-st rev s st arm edges in half to wrong side and catch stitch, then sew on sleeves along these seams. Join side and sleeve seams, joining tucks and hems to form tubes. Sew down pocket linings; fold tops in half to wrong side and catch stitch; sew down ends. Fold collar in half to right side and sew down. Sew on toggles. With four 6-m lengths of C make cord; thread through hem and knot ends.

Summer gold

Day or night you'll get that glow in this simple square-neck sweater that cleverly combines a soft cotton yarn with a metallic thread.

MATERIALS: 4 (4:5:5) 100g hanks Twilleys D42 Dishcloth Cotton (A) and 8 (8:9:10) spools Twilleys Gold Dust 20 (B); 3¼mm (No 10) and 4mm (No 8) knitting needles.

Measurements: To fit 81 (86 : 91 : 97) cm, 32 (34:36:38) inch bust – actual meas, 85 (91:97:103) cm; length, 59 (60:61:62) cm; sleeve, 43 (43:45:45) cm.

Tension: 18 sts to 6 cm; 32 rows (8 patts) to 9 cm.

Abbreviations: See page 7.

BACK: With 3¼mm needles and A cast on 87 (93:99:105) sts. **1st row.** P 1, (k 1 tbl, p 1) to end. **2nd row.** K 1, (p 1 tbl, k 1) to end. Rep last 2 rows 8 times *. **Inc row** (right side). With B k 2, (inc, k 1) to last st, k 1. 129 (138:147:156) sts. Change to 4mm needles. With B p 1 row. Patt thus: **1st row.** With A k 1, (sl 1, k 2) to end, ending last rep k 1. **2nd row.** With A p 1, (sl 1, p 2 tog and do not sl sts off left-hand needle, then p 1st st again and sl both lps off left-hand needle tog) to last 2 sts, sl 1, p 1. **3rd and 4th rows.** With B k 1 row and p 1 row. These 4 rows form patt. Cont in patt until work meas 59 (60:61:62) cm, ending with a 2nd patt row. With B k 1 row, dec 1 st at centre for 2nd and 4th sizes only.

Shoulder Shaping: Next row. With B cast off purlwise 42 (45:48:51) sts, p 45 (47:51:53) sts, cast off purlwise 42 (45:48:51) sts. Leave centre sts on a st-holder.

FRONT: As back until work meas 53 (54:55:56) cm, ending with 3rd patt row. With B p 1 row, dec 1 st at centre for 2nd and 4th sizes only.

Neck Shaping: Next row. Patt 42 (45:48:51) sts, turn. Cont on these sts only. Patt until work meas 59 (60:61:62) cm, ending with a 3rd patt row. With B cast off purlwise. Sl centre 45 (47:51:53) sts on a st-holder, rejoin A at inner end of rem sts and work other side to match.

SLEEVES: With 3¼mm needles and A cast on 41 (41:44:44) sts. Work as back to *. **Inc row.** With B k 2 (2:1:1),

inc, k 1, (inc twice in next st, k 1, inc once in next st, k 1) 9 (9:10:10) times, k 1. 69 (69:75:75) sts. Change to 4mm needles. Patt as back, inc 1 st each end of 3rd and every foll 4th row until there are 79 (79:85:85) sts, then inc 1 st each end of every foll 8th row until there are 105 (105:111:111) sts. Patt straight until work meas 43 (43:45:45) cm, ending with a 3rd patt row. With B cast off purlwise.

NECKBAND: With B join right shoulder seam. With right side facing, using 3¼mm needles and A k up 22 sts down left side of front and 1 st from corner, k sts from st-holder, k up 1 st from corner and 22 sts up right side of front, k back neck sts. 136 (140:148:152) sts **1st row.** (K 1, p 1 tbl) to end. **2nd row.** (Rib as set to within 2 sts of corner st, p 2 tog, k corner st tbl, p 2 tog) twice, rib to end. **3rd row.** (Rib to within 2 sts of corner st, k 2 tog, p corner st tbl, k 2 tog) twice, rib to end. Rep 2nd and 3rd rows 3 times more, then 2nd row again. Still dec at corners, cast off ribwise.

MAKING UP: Press work lightly. Use A to sew rib seams and B for rem seams. Join left shoulder and neckband. Beg and ending 18 (18:19:19) cm from shoulder seams, sew sleeves on sides of back and front. Join side and sleeve seams. Press seams lightly.

Lacy camisole

Show off a tan to perfection when you create this pretty lace patterned, white cotton vest.

MATERIALS: D M C Splendida is no longer available, we suggest using 1 (200g) ball Coats Maxi Pellicano No 5; 2¾mm (No 12) and 3mm (No 11) knitting needles.

Measurements: To fit 86 (91:97) cm, 34 (36:38) inch bust – actual meas, 83 (90:97) cm; length at underarm, 28 cm.

Tension: 20 sts to 7 cm; 24 rows to 6 cm over faggot stitch; each butterfly panel, 3 cm wide.

Abbreviations: See page 7.

Note. – Check count sts after 6th patt rows only – sts in butterfly panels vary on each row.

BACK AND FRONT ALIKE: With 2¾mm needles cast on 105 (113:121) sts. **1st row.** K 1 tbl, (p 1, k 1 tbl) to end. **2nd row.** P 1 tbl, (k 1, p 1 tbl) to end. Rep these 2 rows 8 times more, then 1st row again. **Inc row.** P 4 (5:6), (inc, p 2) to last 2 (3:4) sts, p 2 (3:4). 138 (148:158) sts. Change to 3mm needles. Patt thus: **1st row.** P 1, * p 1, k 2, yfd, k 2 tog tbl *; rep from * to * 4 (5:6) times more, (p 1, k 4, k 2 tog, yfd, k 2 tog tbl, k 4, rep from * to * once) 5 times, rep from * to * 4 (5:6) times, p 2. **2nd row.** K 1, * k 1, p 2, yrn, p 2 tog *; rep from * to * 4 (5:6) times more, (k 1, p 3, p 2 tog tbl, let yfd of previous row sl off left-hand needle, yrn twice, p 2 tog, p 3, rep from * to * once) 5 times, rep from * to * 4 (5:6) times, k 2. These 2 rows form 5 (6:7) faggot st patts at each side and single patts between butterfly panels – now referred to as faggot sts. **3rd row.** P 1, faggot 25 (30:35) sts, (p 1, k 2, k 2 tog, let double yrn of previous row sl off left-hand needle, yfd and over needle 3 times, k 2 tog tbl, k 2, faggot 5 sts) 5 times, faggot 20 (25:30) sts, p 2. **4th row.** K 1, faggot 25 (30:35) sts, (k 1, p 1, p 2 tog tbl, let triple yfd of previous row sl off left-hand needle, yrn 3 times, p 2 tog, p 1, faggot 5 sts) 5 times, faggot 20 (25:30) sts, k 2. **5th row.** P 1, faggot 25 (30:35) sts, (p 1, k 2 tog, let triple yrn of previous row sl off left-hand needle, lp 4 sts on to right-hand needle thus: (hold yarn in left hand and take yarn over and under 1st finger of left hand, insert right-hand needle knitwise into lp on finger and tighten on to needle) 4 times, insert right-hand needle under 4 dropped strands and k 1, yfd and k 1 again, lp 4 more sts on to right-hand needle, k 2 tog tbl, faggot 5 sts) 5 times, faggot 20 (25:30) sts, p 2. **6th row.** K 1, faggot 25 (30:35) sts, (k 1, p 5, p 2 tog, p 6, faggot 5 sts) 5 times, faggot 20 (25:30) sts, k 2. These 6 rows form patt. Cont until 15th patt from beg has been worked.

Armhole Shaping: Cast off 26 (31:36) sts at beg of next 2 rows. Patt straight until 6th row of 18th patt from beg has been worked.

Neck Shaping: Next row. P 1, k 4, k 2 tog, yfd, k 2 tog tbl, k 4, p 1, turn. Cont on these sts only for shoulder strap until 6th row of 27th (28th:29th) patt from beg has been worked. Leave sts on a st-holder. Sl centre 58 sts on a st-holder and work other shoulder strap to match.

SHOULDER JOINS: Sl shoulder strap sts on to 3mm needles with points to inner edges. With right sides of one pair of straps tog and needles parallel, k 1 st from each needle tog while casting off.

NECK EDGINGS: With right side facing, using 2¾mm needles, beg at one shoulder join and k up 53 (59:65) sts down side of neck, k centre sts, k up 53 (59:65) sts up other side of neck to shoulder join. Cast off firmly knitwise. Work other side to match.

ARMHOLE EDGINGS: As neck edging, picking up 192 (214:236) sts around entire armhole.

MAKING UP: Block and press. Taking 1½ sts from each edge into seams, join sides. Join ends of neck edging. Press seams.

The classic collection

hese gentle, fresh sweaters are the sort of classics-with-a-twist that never date. Knit them now in natural cotton, lightweight wool – even luxury angora. Mix classy cables and simple textured stitches in soft pastels and creamy neutral shades for a stunning effect. These sweaters will repay the time and effort you put into knitting them by looking – and feeling – good, time after time.

PALE OPAL

River blue

Ribs and ridges in soft cotton give this sweater a fresh outdoor feel that's also very feminine.

MATERIALS: 16 (17:18) 50g balls Schachenmayr Alpha; 3¾mm (No 9) and 4mm (No 8) knitting needles.

Measurements: To fit 86 (91:97) cm, 34 (36:38) inch bust loosely – actual meas, 109 (113:119) cm; length, 65 (68:71) cm; sleeve, 47 cm.

Tension: 10 sts to 5cm; 14 rows to 5 cm over wide rib; 32 rows to 11 cm over ridge patt.

Abbreviations: See page 7.

BACK: With 3¾mm needles cast on 111 (115:121) sts. Work 4 rows k 1, p 1 rib. Change to 4mm needles and cont in wide rib thus: **1st row** (right side). K. **2nd row.** K 0 (2:2), (p 3, k 3) to last 3 (5:5) sts, p 3, k 0 (2:2). These 2 rows form wide rib. Cont until work meas 38 (40:42) cm from beg, ending with a right side row. Now work in ridge patt for yoke. **1st row** (wrong side). K. **2nd row.** P. **3rd to 8th rows.** Beg p, work 6 rows s st. These 8 rows form ridge patt *. Cont until 2nd (4th:6th) row of 10th ridge patt has been worked.

Neck Shaping: Next row (wrong side). P 43 (45:48), cast off centre 25 sts, p 43 (45:48). Cont on last sts only and cast off 5 sts at beg of foll 2 alt rows. Cast off 33 (35:38) sts. With right side facing, rejoin yarn to inner end of rem sts and work other side of neck to match.

FRONT: As back to *. Cont in ridge patt until 4th (6th:8th) row of 8th patt has been worked.

Neck Shaping: Next row (wrong side). Patt 47 (49:52), cast off centre 17 sts, patt 47 (49:52). Cont on last sts only and cast off 4 sts at beg of next alt row and 2 sts at beg of foll 4 alt rows. Dec 1 st at beg of next 2 alt rows. Work 4 rows. Cast off 33 (35:38) sts. With right side facing, rejoin yarn to inner end of rem sts and work other side of neck to match, reversing shaping.

SLEEVES: With 3¾mm needles cast on 53 (55:57) sts. Work 13 rows k 1, p 1 rib. **Inc row.** Rib 6, inc, * rib 7 (5:4), inc; rep from * 4 (6:8) times, rib 6 (6:5). 59 (63:67) sts. Change to 4mm needles and cont in wide rib thus: **1st row** (right side). K. **2nd row.** K 1 (3:2), (p 3, k 3) to last 4 (6:5) sts, p 3, k 1 (3:2). Cont in wide rib as set and inc 1 st each end of next and every foll 5th row until there are 95 (99:103) sts. Work 3 rows, ending with a right side row. Still inc 1 st each end of 2nd and every 5th row, cont in ridge patt as back yoke until there are 105 (109:113) sts. Work 6 rows, thus completing 4th row of 4th ridge patt. Cast off loosely.

NECKBAND: Join right shoulder. With right side facing, using 3¾mm needles k up 118 sts evenly around neck. Work 7 rows k 1, p 1 rib. Cast off ribwise.

MAKING UP: Press work. Join left shoulder and neckband seam. Beg and ending at beg of ridge patt, sew sleeves to sides. Taking into seams 1 st from each edge on 1st size and a ½ st on 2nd and 3rd sizes, join side and sleeve seams. Press seams.

Cool buttermilk

Pattern a pure wool, boxy sweater with textured triangles for a look that's smart *and* comfortable.

MATERIALS: Copley Vintage Double Knitting is 'no longer available, we suggest using 12 (13) 50g balls Lister Motoravia Superwash DK; 4mm (No 8) knitting needles.

Measurements: To fit 86 to 91 (97 to 102) cm, 34 to 36 (38 to 40) inch bust – actual meas, 103 (113) cm; length, 60 cm; sleeve, 40 cm.

Tension: 12 sts (2 patts) to 5 cm; 36 rows (6 patts) to 11·5 cm.

Abbreviations: See page 7.

BACK: Using thumb method cast on 106 (116) sts. P 2 rows, k 2 rows for welting. **Inc row** (right side). (P 4, inc) to last 6 sts, p 6 *. 126 (138) sts. Patt from chart thus: Read 1st and all wrong side rows from left to right; 2nd and all right side rows from right to left. Rep 6 rows of chart until work meas 59 cm from beg, ending with a 4th patt row.

Shoulder Shaping: Next 2 rows. Patt to last 12 sts, turn. **Next 2 rows.** Patt to last 22 (24) sts, turn. **Next 2 rows.** Patt to last 32 (36) sts, turn. **Next row.** Patt to last 42 (48) sts, turn. **Next row.** K 42 sts for back neck, *do not turn*. Over *next* 42 (48) sts, k 2 rows, p 1 row. Cast off these 42 (48) sts purlwise. Sl 42 back neck sts on to a st-holder. Rejoin yarn and over rem 42 (48) sts, p 2 rows, k 1 row. Cast off knitwise.

FRONT: As back until work meas 51 cm, ending with a 5th patt row.

Neck Shaping: Next row. Patt 42 (48) sts, turn. Cont on these sts only until work meas 59 cm, ending with a 4th patt row **.

Shoulder Shaping: Next 2 rows. Patt to last 12 sts, turn and patt to end. **Next 2 rows.** Patt to last 22 (24) sts, turn and patt to end. **Next 2 rows.** Patt to last 32 (36) sts, turn and patt to end. Over all 42 (48) sts, p 2 rows, k 1 row. Cast off knitwise. Sl centre 42 sts on to a spare needle. Work other side to match to **. Patt 1 row more. Shape shoulder as 1st side, ending k 2 rows, p 1 row. Cast off purlwise.

SLEEVES: Using thumb method cast on 51 (56) sts. Work as back to *. 60 (66) sts. Patt from chart as back, inc 1 st each end of every 4th row until there are 114 (120) sts. Patt 6 rows to complete

19th patt thus ending with a right side row. P 2 rows, k 2 rows, p 2 rows and k 1 row. Cast off knitwise.

NECKBAND: Join right shoulder. K up 20 sts down left side of neck, k sts from spare needle, k up 20 sts up right side of neck and 2 sts down side of back neck, k sts from st-holder, k 2 sts up side of back neck. (128 sts) K 1 row, p 1 row. **Next row.** P 64, p 2 tog, p 2 tog tbl, p 38, p 2 tog, p 2 tog tbl, p 18. **Next row.** K 17, skpo, k 2 tog, k 36, skpo, k 2 tog, k 63. K 1 row. Cast off purlwise.

MAKING UP: Press lightly avoiding welting. Join rem shoulder and neckband seam. Beg and ending 24 (25) cm from shoulders, sew cast-off edge of sleeves to sides. Join sides and sleeves. Press seams lightly.

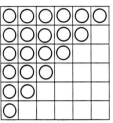

▲ **Begin here**

K on right side; p on wrong.

P on right side; k on wrong.

Marzipan

MATERIALS: Wendy Fiori is no longer available, we suggest using 12 (13:14) 50g balls Pingouin Soda; 4½mm (No 7) and 5½mm (No 5) knitting needles.

Measurements: To fit 81 to 86 (91 to 97:102 to 107) cm, 32 to 34 (36 to 38:40 to 42) inch bust – actual meas, 90 (99:111) cm; length, 64 (65:66) cm; sleeve, 39 (39:40) cm.

Tension: 16 sts (4 patts) to 8·5 cm; 14 rows to 5 cm.

Abbreviations: See page 7.

BACK: With 4½mm needles cast on 87 (95:107) sts. Rib patt thus: **1st row** (right side). K 3, (with yarn at back sl 1 purlwise, k 3) to end. **2nd row.** K 3, (p 1, k 3) to end. These 2 rows form rib patt. Patt 6 rows more. Change to 5½mm needles *. Cont in rib patt until work meas 64 (65:66) cm from beg.

Shoulder Shaping: Cast off 10 (11:13) sts at beg of next 4 rows and 9 (10:11) sts at beg of foll 2 rows. Leave 29 (31:33) sts on a st-holder.

FRONT: As back to *. Cont in rib patt until work meas 55 (56:57) cm from beg, ending with a wrong side row.

Neck Shaping: Next row. Patt 37 (40:45) sts, turn. Cont on these sts only. Dec 1 st at beg of next and foll 7 alt rows. Patt 10 rows straight.

Shoulder Shaping: Cast off 10 (11:13) sts at beg of next and foll alt row. Patt 1 row. Cast off 9 (10:11) sts. Sl 13 (15:17) sts at centre on to a st-holder, and work other side to match.

SLEEVES: With 4½mm needles cast on 47 (51:55) sts. Patt as back to *. Cont in patt, inc 1 st each end of next and every foll 5th row until there are 87 (91:95) sts. Patt straight until work meas 39 (39:40) cm from beg, ending with a wrong side row. Cast off loosely.

NECKBAND: Join right shoulder seam. With right side facing, using 4½mm needles k up 23 sts down left side of front, k sts from st-holder, k up 23 sts up right side of front, k back neck sts, 88 (92:96) sts. Beg p, work 4 rows s st. K 1 row (hemline). Beg k, work 4 rows s st. Cast off very loosely.

MAKING UP: Do not press. Join left shoulder and neckband seam. Fold neckband to wrong side on hemline and catch stitch. Beg and ending 23 (24:25) cm from shoulder seams, sew sleeves on sides of back and front. Join side and sleeve seams. Press seams very lightly.

Sandalwood

This feminine sweater in soft, brushed yarn has gently emphasised shoulders and a pretty twisted rib pattern.

MATERIALS: 8 (8:9) 50g balls Twilleys Featherspun; 3¼mm (No 10) and 4mm (No 8) knitting needles; cable needle; small shoulder pads.

Measurements: To fit 81 (86:91) cm, 32 (34:36) inch bust – actual meas, 89 (94:99) cm; length, 54 cm; sleeve, 46 cm.

Tension: Equivalent to 11 sts, 14 rows to 5 cm over s st; 21 sts of centre feather patt of chart, 7·5 cm wide.

Abbreviations: See page 7.

BACK: With 3¼mm needles cast on 111 (119:127) sts. Cont in rib thus: **1st row.** K 1 tbl, (p 1, k 1 tbl) to end. **2nd row.** P 1 tbl, (k 1, p 1 tbl) to end. Rep these 2 rows 8 times more, then 1st row again. **Inc row.** Rib 3, (inc, p 1 tbl) 1 (2:3) times, rib 10, * inc, p 1 tbl, inc *, rib 21, rep from * to *, rib 11, (inc, p 1 tbl) 3 (5:7) times, rib 10, rep from * to *, rib 21, rep from * to *, rib 11, (inc, p 1 tbl) 1 (2:3) times, rib 2. 124 (136: 148) sts. Change to 4mm needles. Read

key given with chart and cont working from chart thus: **1st row.** Reading from right to left, p 1 st before right-hand dotted line of size required, rep 61 (67:73) sts of 1st row between dotted lines of size required twice, p 1 st beyond left-hand dotted line. **2nd row.** Reading from left to right, k 1 st before left-hand dotted line of size required, rep 61 (67:73) sts of 2nd row between dotted lines of size required twice, k 1 st beyond right-hand dotted line. Cont in this way until each row of chart has been worked. These 28 rows form feather and rib patt. Cont until 2nd (28th: 26th) row of 4th (3rd: 3rd) patt from beg has been worked.

Armhole Shaping: Cast off 9 (11:13) sts at beg of next 2 rows. Dec 1 st each end of next and foll 4 (5:6) alt rows. 96 (102:108) sts **. Patt straight until 24th row of 5th patt has been worked.

Shoulder Shaping: Cast off 9 (10:11) sts at beg of next 4 rows and 9 sts at beg

of foll 2 rows. Leave 42 (44:46) sts on a st-holder.

FRONT: As back to **. Patt straight until 2nd row of 5th patt from beg has been worked.

Neck Shaping: Next row. Patt 38 (40:42), turn. Cont on these sts only. Dec 1 st at neck edge on next and foll 10 alt rows, thus completing 24th row of 5th patt.

Shoulder Shaping: Cast off 9 (10:11) sts at beg of next and foll alt row. Work 1 row. Cast off. Sl centre 20 (22:24) sts on a st-holder, rejoin yarn at inner end of rem sts and work other side to match, reversing shapings.

SLEEVES: With 3¼mm needles cast on 53 sts. Rib 17 (19:21) rows as back. **Inc row.** Rib 3, inc, p 1 tbl, inc, (rib 3, inc) twice, (p 1 tbl, inc) 3 times, rib 3, inc, rib 5, inc, rib 3, (inc, p 1 tbl) 3 times, (inc, rib 3) twice, inc, p 1 tbl, inc, rib 3. (69 sts) Change to 4mm needles. Working from 2nd size only of chart as back (rep sts between dotted lines once), patt 12 (8:4) rows. Now taking extra sts into rib patt of p 2, k 1 tbl rib as set at each side of chart, cont inc 1 st each end of next and every foll 8th (8th:7th) row until there are 89 (93:97) sts. Patt straight until 2nd (28th:26th) row of 5th (4th:4th) patt from beg has been worked. To shape top cast off 9 (11:13)

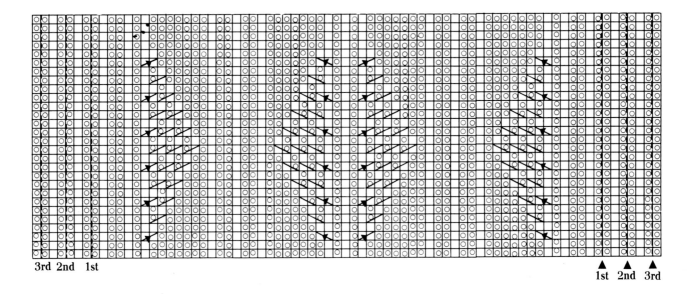

3rd 2nd 1st   ▲ ▲ ▲   **1st 2nd 3rd**

⊡ P on right side rows; k on wrong side rows.

☐ K tbl on right side rows; p tbl on wrong side rows.

⟍ Sl 1 st on cable needle and leave at front, k next st, k tbl st from cable needle.

⟋ Sl 1 st on cable needle and leave at back, k tbl next st, k st from cable needle.

⟍ Sl 1 st on cable needle and leave at front, p next st, k tbl st from cable needle.

⟋ Sl 1 st on cable needle and leave at back, k tbl next st, p st from cable needle.

sts at beg of next 2 rows. Dec 1 st each end of next and every alt row until 47 sts rem. Working feather patt at centre only and rib at sides as set, patt 11 (13:15) rows straight. Dec 1 st each end of every row until 35 sts rem. **Next row.** (K 2 tog, p 1) 4 times, (k 2 tog) twice, sl 1, k 2 tog, psso, (k 2 tog tbl) twice, (p 1, k 2 tog tbl) 4 times. **Next row.** P 1, (p 2 tog) to end. Cast off.

NECKBAND: Join right shoulder. With 3¼mm needles k up 28 (29:29) sts down left side of front, across centre sts: (p 1, k 1 tbl) 3 (2:1) times, (p 2 tog, k 1 tbl) 2 (4:6) times, p 2 tog, (k 1 tbl, p 1) 3 (2:1) times, k up 28 (29:29) sts up right side of front, across back sts: p 0 (1:0), k tbl 1 (1:0), (p 2 tog, k 1 tbl) 2 (1:1) times, p 7, k 1 tbl, p 1 (k 1 tbl, p 2 tog) 3 (5:7) times, k 1 tbl, p 1,

k 1 tbl, p 7, (k 1 tbl, p 2 tog) 2 (1:1) times, k tbl 1 (1:0), p 0 (1:0). Beg 3 sizes p 1 tbl (k 1:k 1) and working 1st row as wrong side rib row of back, rib 15 rows. Cast off loosely ribwise.

MAKING UP: Join left shoulder and neckband seam. Fold neckband in half to wrong side and catch stitch. Set in sleeves. Join side and sleeve seams. Sew in shoulder pads.

Pale opal

If you're treating yourself to the luxury of angora, choose this classic, cabled sweater – then sit back and enjoy the compliments.

MATERIALS: 16 (18) 20g balls Jaeger Angora Spun; 2¾mm (No 12) and 4mm (No 8) knitting needles; cable needle; shoulder pads.

Measurement: To fit 86 (91) cm, 34 (36) inch bust – actual meas, 95 (100) cm; length, 57 (59) cm; sleeve, 44 cm.

Tension: 25 (27) sts (1 patt) to 8 (8·5) cm; 17 rows to 5 cm.

Abbreviations: See page 7.

BACK: With 2¾mm needles cast on 133 (143) sts. **1st rib row.** (K 1 tbl, p 1) to last st, k 1 tbl. **2nd rib row.** (P 1, k 1 tbl) to last st, p 1. These 2 rows form rib. Rep them 10 times more, then work 1st row again. **Inc row.** Inc, rib 10, * inc, rib 10 (11), inc twice in next st, rib 10 (11); rep from * to last 12 sts, inc, rib 10, inc **. 151 (161) sts. Change to 4mm needles. Work patt from chart, reading 1st and all right side rows from right to left and 2nd and all wrong side rows from left to right thus: **1st row** (right side). P 5, * work 16 sts of 1st row of chart, p 9 (11); rep from * to end, ending last rep p 5. **2nd row.** K 5, * work 16 sts of 2nd row of chart, k 9 (11); rep from * to end, ending last rep k 5. Cont in this way until chart is completed. These 12 rows form patt. Cont until 8th row of 8th patt has been worked.

Armhole Shaping: Cast off 26 (27) sts at beg of next 2 rows ***. Cont straight until 8th (2nd) row of 15th (16th) patt has been worked.

Shoulder Shaping: Cast off 13 (14) sts at beg of next 4 rows. Leave 47 (51) sts.

FRONT: As back to ***.

Neck Shaping: Next row. Patt 49 (53) sts, turn. Cont on these sts only. Dec 1 st at neck edge on next and every foll 3rd row until 26 (28) sts rem. Cont straight until 8th (2nd) row of 15th (16th) patt has been worked.

Shoulder Shaping: Cast off 13 (14) sts at beg of next and foll alt row. Sl centre st on to a safety pin. Complete other side of neck to match.

SLEEVES: With 2¾mm needles cast on 89 (95) sts. Work as back to **. 101 (107) sts. Change to 4mm needles. Cont in patt as back and inc 1 st each end of 3rd and every foll 5th row until there are 143 (149) sts. Inc 1 st each end of every 4th row until there are 153 (161) sts. Cont until 12th (2nd) row of 13th (14th) patt has been worked. Cast off.

NECKBAND: Join right shoulder. With right side facing, using 2¾mm needles k up 75 (79) sts down left side of neck, k centre st from safety pin, k up 75 (79) sts up right side and k sts of back. 198 (210) sts. **1st row.** (P 1, k 1 tbl) to within 2 sts of centre st, p 2 tog, p centre st, p 2 tog tbl, k 1 tbl, (p 1, k1 tbl) to end. **2nd row.** (P 1, k 1 tbl) to within 2 sts of centre st, skpo, k 1 tbl, k 2 tog, k 1 tbl, (p 1, k1 tbl) to end. Rep last 2 rows 8 times. Cast off ribwise.

MAKING UP: Do not press. Join left shoulder and neckband seam. Setting 8 (8·5) cm of sides of sleeves to cast off groups at armholes, set in sleeves. Join sides and sleeves. Sew in shoulder pads.

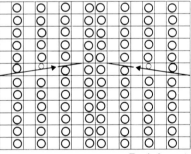

Begin here ▲

☐
K tbl on right side; p tbl on wrong.

Ⓞ
P on right side; k on wrong.

Sl 3 sts on to cable needle and leave at front, (k 1, p 1) twice, rib sts as set from cable needle.

Sl 4 sts on to cable needle and leave at back, rib 3 sts as set, (p 1, k 1) twice from cable needle.

Classy cream

Huge shoulder pads and an unusual zigzag cable on rib give this long-line jacket lots of style.

MATERIALS: Wendy Shetland Chunky is no longer available, we suggest using 22 (23) 50g balls Sirdar Sovereign Chunky; 5½mm (No 5) and 6½mm (No 3) knitting needles; cable needle; 4 buttons; shoulder pads.

Measurements: To fit 86 to 91 (97 to 102) cm, 34 to 36 (38 to 40) inch bust – actual meas, 110 (120) cm; length, 75 cm; sleeve, 46 cm.

Tension: 16 sts, 20 rows to 10 cm over rib when pressed.

Abbreviations: See page 7.

Note. – For symmetrical zigzag, right side of back and left front begin on 1st row of chart and 1st to 52nd rows form pattern; left side of back and right front begin on 27th row then 27th to 52nd rows and 1st to 26th rows form pattern.

BACK: With 5½mm needles cast on 96 (104) sts. **Next row.** (P 2, k 2) 8 (9) times, p 5, (k 2, p 2) 5 times, k 2, p 5, (k 2, p 2) 8 (9) times. Patt thus: **1st row** (right side). (K 2, p 2) 2 (3) times, reading from right to left patt 29 sts of 1st row of chart, (p 2, k 2) 5 times, p 2, reading from right to left patt 29 sts of 27th row of chart, (p 2, k 2) 2 (3) times. **2nd row.** (P 2, k 2) 2 (3) times, reading from left to right patt 29 sts of 28th row of chart, (k 2, p 2) 5 times, k 2, reading from left to right patt 29 sts of 2nd row of chart, (k 2, p 2) 2 (3) times. Work 4 rows more. Change to 6½mm needles. Cont in patt until 26 chart rows have been worked. **Next row.** Rib 8 (12), patt 29 sts of 27th row of chart, rib 22, patt

29 sts of 1st row of chart, rib 8 (12). Cont in patt until 52 chart rows have been worked. These 52 rows form patt. Cont in patt for 52 rows more.

Armhole Shaping: Cast off 7 sts at beg of next 2 rows. Cont in patt until 46th row of 3rd patt from beg has been worked.

Shoulder Shaping: Cast off 10 (12) sts at beg of next 4 rows and 11 sts at beg of foll 2 rows. Cast off rem 20 sts ribwise.

LEFT FRONT: With 5½mm needles cast on 58 (62) sts. **Next row.** K 5, (p 2, k 2) 4 times, p 5, (k 2, p 2) 8 (9) times. Patt thus: **1st row** (right side). (K 2, p 2) 2 (3) times, reading from right to left patt 29 sts of 1st row of chart, (p 2, k 2) 4 times, then for border p 2, k 3. **2nd row.** For border k 5, then (p 2, k 2) 4 times, reading from left to right patt 29 sts of 2nd row of chart, (k 2, p 2) 2 (3) times. Working 5 border sts as set, work 4 rows more. Change to 6½mm needles. Cont until 2nd patt has been worked.

Armhole Shaping: Cast off 7 sts at beg of next row. Cont in patt until 34th row of 3rd patt from beg has been worked.

Neck Shaping: 1st row. Patt 30 (34), k 21. **2nd row.** K 21, patt 30 (34). **3rd row.** As 1st. Cast off 20 sts at beg of next row, patt to end. 31 (35) sts. Keeping 1 st at neck k on every row, patt 8 rows.

Shoulder Shaping: Cast off 10 (12) sts at beg of next and foll alt row. Work 1 row. Cast off.

RIGHT FRONT: With 5½mm needles cast on 58 (62) sts. **Next row.** (P 2, k 2) 8 (9) times, p 5, (k 2, p 2) 4 times, k 5. **1st row** (right side). For border k 3, p 2, then (k 2, p 2) 4 times, reading from right to left patt 29 sts of 27th row of chart, (p 2, k 2) 2 (3) times. **2nd row.** (P 2, k 2) 2 (3) times, reading from left to right patt 29 sts of 28th row of chart, (k 2, p 2) 4 times, then for border k 5.

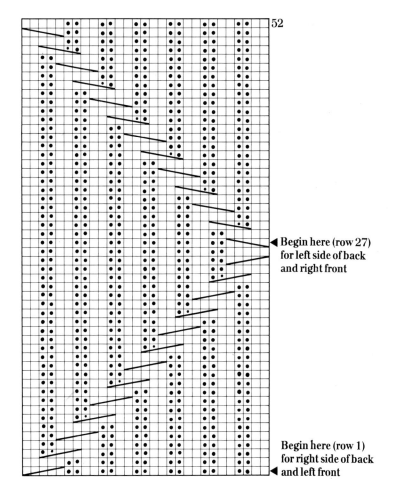

52

◄ **Begin here (row 27) for left side of back and right front**

Begin here (row 1) for right side of back and left front ◄

☐

K on right side; p on wrong.

⬤

P on right side; k on wrong.

Sl next 2 sts on cable needle and leave at back, k 3, then k 2 from cable needle.

As above but p 2 from cable needle.

Sl next 3 sts on cable needle and leave at front, k 2, then k 3 from cable needle.

As above but p 2 instead of k 2.

CLASSY CREAM

Working 5 border sts as set, work 4 rows. Change to 6½mm needles. Cont until 38 patt rows have been worked. **Buttonhole row.** Patt 4, cast off 3, patt 10, cast off 3, patt to end. **Next row.** Patt to end casting on 3 sts over those cast off. Patt 28 rows; rep buttonhole rows. Patt as set and complete as left front, reversing shapings.

SLEEVES: With 5½mm needles cast on 34 sts. Work 9 rows p 2, k 2 rib. Change to 6½mm needles. Cont in rib and inc

1 st each end of next and every foll 4th row until there are 76 sts. Cont until work meas 51 cm. Cast off ribwise.

COLLAR: With 5½mm needles cast on 18 sts. **Next row** (wrong side). (P 2, k 2) 4 times, p 2. Cont in rib and cast on 4 sts at beg of next 8 rows and 5 sts at beg of next 2 rows, taking extra sts into rib patt. (60 sts) Change to 6½mm needles. Rib 18 rows. Leave sts. With right side facing and using 6½mm needles k up 16 sts up right-hand straight side edge of

collar, rib across collar sts, k up 16 sts down left-hand straight side edge of collar. K 1 row. **Next row.** K 16, inc, k 58, inc, k 16. K 1 row. Cast off loosely.

MAKING UP: Press work. Join shoulder seams. Sew on collar, joining shaped side edges to cast-off edges on fronts for 9 cm leaving 5 cm free on both edges for revers. Setting 10 rows at sides of sleeves to armhole edges, set in sleeves. Join side and sleeve seams. Sew on buttons. Sew in pads.

Rich camel

Relax in this long sweater – it's a subtle combination of cable and stocking stitch.

MATERIALS: 8 (8:9) 100g balls King Cole Superspun Superwash Double Knitting; 3¼mm (No 10) and 4mm (No 8) knitting needles; cable needle.

Measurements: To fit 76 to 81 (86 to 91:97 to 102) cm, 30 to 32 (34 to 36: 38 to 40) inch bust – actual meas, 103 (116:129) cm; length, 66 cm; sleeve, 42 cm.

Tension: 16 sts (1 patt) to 6·5 cm; 32 rows to 10 cm when pressed.

Abbreviations: See page 7.

BACK: With 3¼mm needles cast on 113 (127:141) sts. **M st row.** K 1, (p 1, k 1) to end. Rep m st row 13 times more. Change to 4mm needles. **Inc row.** K 3, *(p 1, k 1) twice, (inc) twice, p 1, k 1, p 1, k 5 *, rep from * to * 6 (7:8) times more, (p 1, k 1) twice, (inc) twice, p 1, k 1, p 1, k 3. 129 (145:161) sts. Patt thus: **1st row** (wrong side). P 4, (k 1, p 7) to last 5 sts, k 1, p 4. **2nd row.** K 3, (p 1, k 1, p 1, k 5) to last 6 sts, p 1, k 1, p 1, k 3. **3rd row.** As 1st. **4th row.** K 3, (p 1, k 1, p 1, sl next 3 sts on cable needle and leave at front, k 2, k sts from cable needle – referred to as c 5, p 1, k 1, p 1, k 5) to last 14 sts, p 1, k 1, p 1, c 5, p 1, k 1, p 1, k 3. **5th to 8th rows.** Rep 1st and 2nd rows twice. These 8 rows form patt. Cont in patt until 5th row of 15th patt from beg has been worked.

Armhole Shaping: Next 2 rows. While working first 10 sts patt 6, (take 2 tog) twice, *at the same time* cast off these 8 rem sts, then patt to end. 109 (125: 141) sts **. Cont straight until work meas 65 cm, ending with a 5th patt row.

Neck Shaping: Next row. Patt 38 (42:50), turn. Cont on these sts only. Cast off 2 (3:3) sts at beg of next row and 2 sts at beg of foll alt row. Cast off rem 34 (37:45) sts, dec 2 sts over each cable as before. Sl 33 (41:41) sts at centre on a st-holder, rejoin yarn to

inner end of rem sts and complete to match other side.

FRONT: As back to **. Cont straight until work meas 60 cm from beg, ending with a 5th patt row.

Neck Shaping: Next row. Patt 45 (51:59), turn. Cont on these sts only. Cast off 4 (5:5) sts at beg of next and foll alt row and 3 (4:4) sts at beg of foll alt row. 34 (37:45) sts. Cont straight until work meas 66 cm from beg, ending with a 1st patt row. Cast off, dec 2 sts over each cable as before. Sl 19 (23:23) sts at centre on a st-holder, rejoin yarn to inner end of rem sts and complete to match other side.

SLEEVES: With 3¼mm needles cast on 51 sts. Work 14 rows m st as back. Change to 4mm needles. **Inc row.** K 3, *(p 1, k 1) twice, (inc) twice *, rep from * to * 6 times more, p 1, k 1, p 1, k 3.

(65 sts). Cont in patt as back and *at the same time* inc 1 st each end of every 3rd row until there are 141 sts. Cont straight until 5th row of 17th patt from beg has been worked. Cast off loosely.

NECKBAND: Join right shoulder seam. With right side facing, using 3¼mm needles k up 27 (31:31) sts down left side of front; across centre sts beg p 1 and work in m st; k up 27 (31:31) sts up right side of front and 7 (9:9) sts down right side of back; across centre sts beg k 1 and work in m st; k up 7 (9:9) sts up left side of back. 120 (144:144) sts. Beg p 1 work 29 rows m st. Cast off loosely.

MAKING UP: Press work. Join left shoulder and neckband seam, reversing seam for final 4 cm of neckband. Setting 3 cm at sides of sleeves to cast-off edges at armholes, set in sleeves. Join side and sleeve seams. Press seams.

Wild orchid

This cool cotton sweater has a light, summery feel with bands of textured stitches and rows of eyelets.

MATERIALS: 9 (10:11) 50g balls Twilleys Stalite Perléspun No. 3; 2¾mm (No 12) and 3¼mm (No 10) knitting needles; 1 button.

Measurements: To fit 83 (91:99) cm, 33 (36:39) inch bust – actual meas, 92 (100:108) cm; length, 54 cm; sleeve, 47 cm.

Tension: 10 sts (1 patt) to 4 cm; 32 rows (1 patt) to 9 cm.

Abbreviations: See page 7.

BACK: With 2¾mm needles cast on 102 (110:118) sts. Work 10 cm k 2, p 2 rib. **Inc row.** P 1 (6:4), inc, * p 6 (5:5), inc; rep from * 13 (15:17) times, p 2 (7:5). 117 (127:137) sts. Change to 3¼mm needles. Cont in patt from chart thus: **1st row** (right side). K as shown on chart. **2nd row.** K 3, p as shown on chart to last 3 sts, k 3. **3rd row.** K 3, reading 3rd row of chart from right to left, work st before dotted line, rep 10 sts beyond dotted line to last 3 sts, k 3. **4th row.** K 3, reading 4th row of chart from left to right, rep 10 sts before dotted line to last 4 sts, work st beyond dotted line, k 3. Cont working each row of chart in this way. These 32 rows form patt *. Patt until 28th row of 5th patt from beg has been worked. Cast off.

FRONT: As back to *. Patt until 6th row of 5th patt from beg has been worked.

Neck Shaping: Next row. Patt 45 (49:53), cast off 27 (29:31) sts, patt to end. Dec 1 st at neck edge on every row until 39 (43:47) sts rem. Cont straight until 28th row of 5th patt from beg has been worked. Cast off. Work other side to match.

SLEEVES: With 2¾mm needles cast on 54 sts. Work 10 cm k 2, p 2 rib. **Inc row.** (P 3, inc) 13 times, p 2. (67 sts) Change to 3¼mm needles. Patt 4 rows as given for back. **5th row.** K 3, pick up strand lying between needles and k it tbl – referred to as m 1, patt to last 3 sts, m 1, k 3. Cont in patt and inc in this way on every foll 4th row until there are 129 sts, working extra sts into patt within 3-st g st borders at each side. Patt 5 rows thus completing 2nd row of 5th patt. P 1 row (right side). Cast off.

NECKBAND: Join right shoulder, matching cast-off sts of front to corresponding sts of back. With right side facing, using 2¾mm needles, k up 28 sts down left side of front, 27 (29:31) sts across centre, 28 sts up right side of front, 39 (41:43) sts across back neck, leaving 39 (43:47) sts at end of cast-off edge of back for left shoulder, cast on 4 sts for underwrap. 126 (130:134) sts. Beg 1st row p 2, work 2 rows k 2, p 2 rib. **Buttonhole row.** Rib to last 3 sts, yrn, p 2 tog, p 1. Rib 3 rows. Cast off ribwise.

MAKING UP: Press work. Join left shoulder seam, omitting neckband. Sew button on underwrap. Beg and ending 26 cm from shoulder seams, sew sleeves on sides of back and front. Join side and sleeve seams. Press seams.

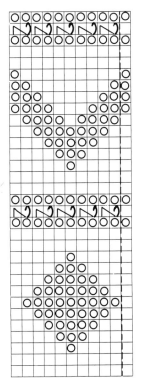

Begin here ▲

☐
K on right side; p on wrong (ie s st).

Ⓞ
P on right side; k on wrong.

⌇
Yfd between sts.

◨
Skpo.

Treasures of the Americas

f you'd like to travel with your knitting needles come with us and explore the exciting motifs used by the Indians of North and South America to decorate beadwork, jewellery, pottery and textiles. Choose authentic earth tones or vivid, clashing colours. Take inspiration from the wide prairies or the mountains of Peru. In these richly patterned knits you'll be noticed wherever you go.

INCA PINK

Inca pink

This huge, chunky sweater is almost long enough to be a dress! The round yoke and bright colours echo vivid South American costumes.
The leggings may look wild but, because they're knitted in the round, creating the sizzling patterns is easier than you might think.

SWEATER

MATERIALS: Studio Yarns Samband Lopi: 6 (100g) balls main colour pink (A) and 1 ball each 2nd colour yellow (B), 3rd colour blue (C), 4th colour green (D) and 5th colour navy (E); 4mm (No 8) and 5½mm (No 5) knitting needles; 6mm (No 4) circular knitting needle, 80 cm long; a set of four 4mm (No 8) double-pointed knitting needles.

Measurements: To fit 81 to 97 cm, 32 to 38 inch bust – actual meas, 118 cm; length, 68 cm; sleeve, 31 cm.

Tension: 15 sts, 21 rows to 10 cm over s st; 16 sts, 16 rows to 10 cm over multi-colour patt.

Abbreviations: See page 7.

Note. – When working multi-colour patterns, do not use the weaving method but strand the yarn not in use loosely across the wrong side of the work, spreading the last few stitches worked to tension the yarn loosely and avoid puckering.

BACK AND FRONT (alike): With 4mm needles and A cast on 85 sts. Work 18 rows k 1, p 1 rib. Change to 5½mm needles. Beg k, cont in s st, inc 1 st each end of 31st row and every foll 10th row until there are 91 sts. Work 9 rows straight.

Underarm Shaping: Cast off 6 sts at beg of next 2 rows. Dec 1 st each end of next 2 rows. Leave 75 sts on a st-holder.

SLEEVES: With 4mm needles and A cast on 37 sts. Work 10 rows k 1, p 1 rib. Change to 5½mm needles. Cont in s st, inc 1 st each end of 3rd and every foll alt row until there are 91 sts. P 1 row.

Underarm Shaping: As back and front.

YOKE: With right side of all parts facing, slip sts of back, one sleeve, front and second sleeve on to circular needle. (300 sts) Cont in rounds thus: Mark beg of round with loop of contrast yarn and slip this loop on every round. Work in s st patt from chart 1 (see note on stranding multi-colour knitting) thus: Reading each line of chart from right to left, rep 6 sts to end for each round. **6th dec round.** With E (k 2 tog, k 21, k 2 tog tbl) to end. (276 sts) Now cont in s st, working patt and decs from chart 2 thus: **For first 7 rounds** read chart from right to left and rep 23 sts of chart to end. **8th round.** With C (k 2 tog as shown by indent on chart, 3 C, 7 B, 3 C, 5 B, 1 C, with C k 2 tog tbl) to end. (252 sts) **For next 7 rounds** rep 21 sts of chart. **16th round.** * With E k 2 tog, (1 D, 1 E) 8 times, 1 D, with E k 2 tog tbl, with D k 2 tog, (1 E, 1 D) 8 times, 1 E, with D k 2 tog tbl; rep from * to end. (228 sts) Cont working as set, dec in first and last colours at edge of indents on 24th and 30th rows of chart, until chart is completed. (180 sts) Cont with A only. **Next round.** (K 2 tog, k 11, k 2 tog tbl) to end. Work 1 round. Working 2 sts less between decs, cont dec in this way on next and foll 2 alt rounds. (84 sts) Change to 4mm double-pointed needles and work 10 rounds k 1, p 1 rib. With 6mm needle cast off ribwise.

MAKING UP: Press work. Take 1 st from each edge into seams. Join underarm seams. Join sides and sleeves. Press seams.

Chart 2

Chart 1

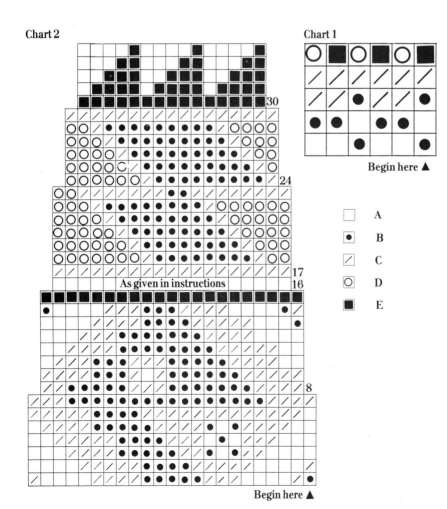

Begin here ▲

As given in instructions

Begin here ▲

	A
●	B
/	C
○	D
■	E

LEGGINGS

MATERIALS: Patons Beehive DK: 2 (50g) balls 1st colour pink (A) and 1 ball each 2nd colour yellow (B), 3rd colour blue (C), 4th colour green (D) and 5th colour dark red (E); sets of four 3¼mm (No 10) and 3¾mm (No 9) double-pointed knitting needles.

Size: Width, average; length, 67 cm.

Tension: 14 sts, 15 rows to 5 cm.

Abbreviations: See page 7.

Note.– When working multi-colour pattern, strand the yarn not in use loosely across the wrong side of the work, spreading the last few stitches worked to tension the yarn loosely.

LEGGINGS (both alike): Beg at ankle. With 3¼mm needles and A cast on 60 sts. (20 sts on each of 3 needles). Working with 4th needle and taking care not to twist cast-on edge on 1st round, cont in rounds of k 1, p 1 rib for 10 cm. Change to 3¾mm needles. **1st inc round.** With A (k 5, pick up strand lying between needles and k it tbl – referred to as m 1) 12

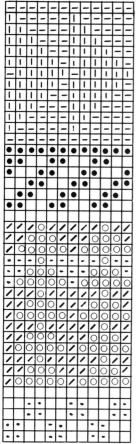

Key 1

☐	A
⊡	B
◎	C
〡	A
●	C
⊘	D
☒	E

Key 2

☐	B
⊡	C
◎	D
〡	A
●	E
⊘	A
⊟	C

Begin here ▲

times. (72 sts) Cont in s st (k every round) and using key 1, work in patt from chart (see note on stranding colour knitting) thus: Reading from right to left rep each line of chart 6 times for each round. Cont until 40 rounds of chart have been worked. **2nd inc round.** With B (k 6, m 1) 12 times. (84 sts) Using key 2, rep each line of chart 7 times for each round and work 40 rounds of chart again.

3rd inc round. With A (k 7, m 1) 12 times. (96 sts) Using key 1, rep each line of chart 8 times for each round and work 40 rounds of chart again. **4th inc round.** With B (k 8, m 1) 12 times. (108 sts) Using key 2, rep each line of chart 9 times for each round and work 40 rounds of chart again. Change to 3¼mm needles. With A work 8 rounds k 1, p 1 rib. Cast off loosely ribwise. Press lightly.

Bolivian blue

Luxuriate in this wonderfully patterned edge-to-edge jacket.

MATERIALS: Sunbeam Paris Luxury Mohair: 4 (50g) balls 1st colour navy (A), 3 balls 2nd colour mauve (B), 2 balls 3rd colour blue (C), 1 ball each 4th colour green (D), 5th colour gold (E), 6th colour pink (F); 5½mm (No 5) and 6½mm (No 3) knitting needles; 5½mm (No 5) circular needle, 100 cm long.

Measurements: To fit up to 107 cm, 42 inch bust – actual meas, all round 133 cm; length, 65 cm; sleeve, 38 cm.

Tension: 15 sts, 16 rows to 10 cm.

Abbreviations: See page 7.

Note. – While working multi-colour knitting, avoid thickening and distorting the fabric over large areas of colour by using a separate small ball of yarn for each block of colour, twisting the yarns together on wrong side when changing colour to avoid holes. For small areas of colour and repeating designs of a few stitches, strand the yarn not in use loosely across the wrong side of the work, spreading the last few stitches worked to tension the yarn loosely and avoid puckering. A combination of both methods may be used where small broken areas of colour occur between large areas and in sections where otherwise it would be necessary to strand more than one colour at a time.

BACK: With 5½mm needles and A cast on 97 sts. **1st row** (right side). K 1 A, (1 C, 1 A) to end. Cont thus, stranding yarns on wrong side of work: **2nd row.** P 1 A, (k 1 C, p 1 A) to end. **3rd row.** K 1 A, (p 1 C, k 1 A) to end. **4th row.** As 2nd. Rep last 2 rows twice more. Change to 6½mm needles. Beg k, cont in s st thus: ** Work 2 rows C. Now cont working patt from chart 1 (see note on colour knitting) thus: Reading 1st and all right side rows from right to left, rep sts before broken line to last st, k st beyond broken line; reading 2nd and all wrong side rows from left to right, p st before broken line, rep sts beyond broken line to end. Cont until chart is completed **. Work 3 rows A. Work 4-row patt from chart 2 as given for chart 1. Work stripes of 2 rows B, 2 rows C, 1 row D, 3 rows B ***. Now work 23-row patt from chart 3 thus: **1st row.** Reading 1st row of chart from right to left, working background circles throughout with B, rep 16 sts before broken line working dot symbol with A for first rep and F, E *, A, F and E for subsequent reps to last st, k st beyond broken line. **2nd row.** Reading 2nd row of chart from left to right, p st before broken line, rep 16 sts beyond broken line while working dot symbol with E for first rep and F, A*, E, F and A for subsequent reps to end. Cont in this way until chart is completed. Work 3 rows B, 1 row D, 2 rows C and 1 row E ****. Cont working from chart 4 (ignore stepped dotted line) thus: **1st row.** Reading from right to left, work 1st row of complete chart, then reading from left to right, beg at * beyond broken line and work back to right-hand edge. Cont working each line of chart in this way. Work 7 rows A.***** **Next row.** P 1 A, (1 C, 1 A) to end. Rep from ** to ** once *****. Work 4 rows A. Rep from ***** to ***** once. Work 1 row A.

Shoulder Shaping: Cont with A only and shape thus: K 84, turn; p 71, turn; k 59, turn; p 47, turn; k 35, turn; cast off 23 sts for back neck and leave 2 sets of 37 sts on st-holders for shoulders.

LEFT FRONT: With 5½mm needles and A cast on 49 sts. Work as back to ***. Now work 23-row patt from chart 3 thus: **1st row.** As 1st row of chart 3 of back to *, k st beyond broken line. **2nd row.** As 2nd row of chart 3 of back to *. Cont in this way until chart is completed. Work 3 rows B.

Front Shaping: While dec 1 st at end of next and every alt row *at the same time,* work 1 row D, 2 rows C and 1 row E **. Cont working from chart 4 thus: **1st row.** Reading 1st row of chart from right to left, patt to within 1 st of stepped dotted line, k 2 tog A. **2nd row.** Reading 2nd row of chart from left to right, beg at stepped dotted line and patt to end. Cont in this way dec 1 st at end of next and every

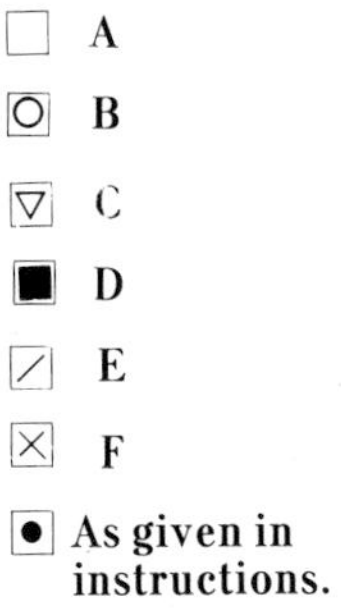

Chart 1

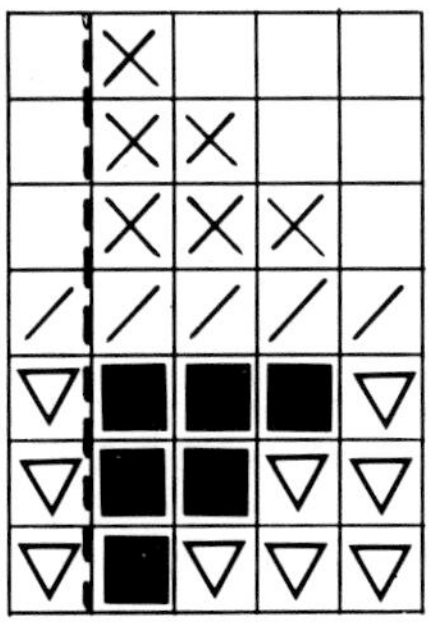

Begin here ▲

Chart 2

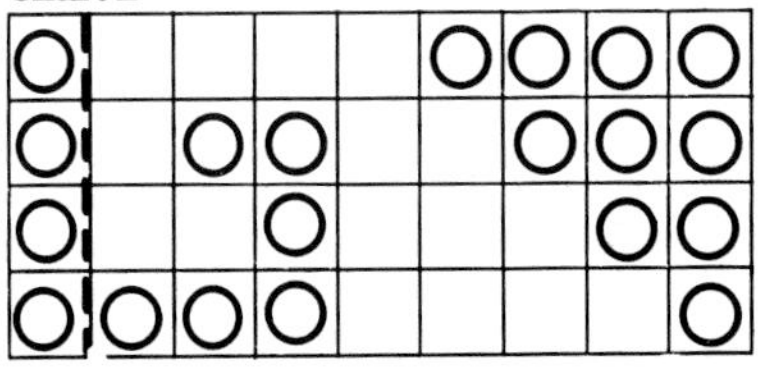

Begin here ▲

Chart 3

Begin here ▲

- ☐ A
- ⊙ B
- ▽ C
- ■ D
- ⧄ E
- ⊠ F
- ● As given in instructions.

alt row as shown by indents of dotted line until chart is completed. Still dec as set work 7 rows A. (37 sts) Cont straight and work from ***** to ***** of back once, work 4 rows A, then work from ***** to ***** again. Work 2 rows A.

Shoulder Shaping: Cont with A only and shape thus: P 24, turn; k to end. P 12, turn; k to end. Leave sts.

RIGHT FRONT: As left to front shaping.

Front Shaping: Dec at beg instead of end, work as left front to **. Cont working from chart 4 thus: **1st row.** Reading 1st row of chart from *left to right* beg at dotted stepped line and with A k 2 tog, k 9 A, 23 F, 13 A. **2nd row.** Reading 2nd row of chart from right to left p from right-hand edge to dotted stepped line. Complete chart; then complete as left front, working 1 row A before shoulder shaping.

SLEEVES: With 5½mm needles and A cast on 49 sts. While working as back to ***, inc 1 st each end of 1st row of chart 1 and every foll 3rd row until there are 65 sts. Now work 23-row patt from chart 3 thus: **1st row.** As 1st row of chart 3 of back to *, then rep 16 sts again with A for dot symbol, k st beyond dotted line. **2nd row.** As 2nd row of chart 3 of back, but work first 16 sts with A for dot symbol, then with E, F and A. Work from chart as set and *at the same time,* inc 1 st each end of 2nd and every foll 4th row until there are 75 sts and chart is completed. Cont working 2 more incs and work as back to ****. With A work 2 rows. Cast off loosely.

FRONT BAND: With circular needle and A cast on 245 sts. Work 1st to 4th rows of back. Rep last 2 rows once more. With C cast off loosely.

MAKING UP: Sl sts of left back and front shoulders on to spare needles

with points to neck edge. With wrong side of back and front tog and needles parallel, using 6½mm needle and A k 1 st from each needle tog while casting off loosely. Join right shoulder to match. Beg and ending 26 cm from shoulder seams, sew sleeves on sides of back and fronts. Join side and sleeve seams. Sew on cast-off edge of front band.

Chart 4

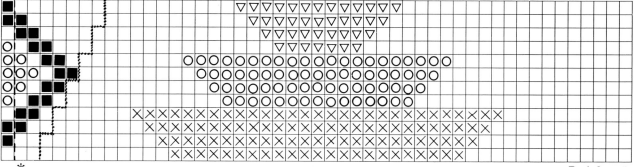

*   **Begin here ▲**

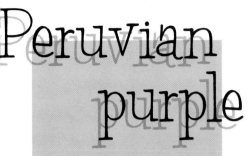

Peruvian purple

This wide, square-neck sweater has striped centre panels. The side and sleeve panels are worked in one.

SWEATER

MATERIALS: Rowan Pure New Wool DK: 10 (25g) skeins 1st colour purple (A), 4 skeins each 2nd colour navy (B), 3rd colour red (C), 4th colour clover (D) and 3 skeins 5th colour green (E): 3¼mm (No 10) and 3¾mm (No 9) knitting needles.
Measurements: To fit 81 to 91 cm, 32 to 36 inch bust – actual meas, 122 cm; length, 49 cm; sleeve, 41 cm.

Tension: Over patt of centre panels, 12 sts to 4 cm and 23 rows to 8 cm. Over patt of side panels and sleeves, 20 sts to 7 cm and 13 rows to 4 cm.
Abbreviations: See page 7.
Note. – When working 2-colour knitting, strand the yarn not in use loosely across the wrong side of the work, spreading the last few stitches worked to tension the yarn loosely and avoid puckering.
CENTRE BACK PANEL: With 3¼mm needles and A cast on 80 sts. Using 3¼mm needles for 1st and 9th rows only and 3¾mm needles for rem rows of chart 1, read k rows from right to left and p rows from left to right and cont in s st thus: Beg k, work 16 rows of chart 1 8 times. With A cast off loosely.
CENTRE FRONT PANEL: Working 16 rows of chart 1 7 times instead of 8, work as centre back panel.
SLEEVE AND SIDE PANELS (2 alike): With 3¼mm needles and A cast on 57 sts. Work 12 rows k 1, p 1 rib. Using 3¼mm needles for 1st and 9th to 12th rows and 3¾mm needles for 2nd to 8th rows of chart 2, reading each row from right to left, cont in s st, noting colour changes on every 12-row rep of chart as given by 6 keys and work 2 rows. Working extra sts

at each end into 8-st patt at each end of chart, inc 1 st each end of next and every foll alt row until there are 175 sts. Work 1 row thus completing 12th row of 10th rep of chart 2.
Side Shaping: Cont in patt as set and cast on 45 sts at beg of next 2 rows. (265 sts) Cont straight until 9th row of 15th rep of chart 2 from beg has been worked. With wrong side facing, using B, cast off knitwise.
MAKING UP: Press work. With k ridges of cast-off edges of sleeve and side panels to right side of work, sew all 16 8-st patts at one end of each to sides of centre back panel. Leaving 9-st centre patt and next 2 8-st patts free, sew remainder of edges to sides of centre front panel.
Neckband: With 3¼mm needles and A k up 53 sts across cast-off edge of back. Work 1 row k 1, p 1 rib. Cont in rib and dec 1 st each end of next 4 rows. Cast off ribwise. Work front neckband to match, then k up 17 sts along side edges of neck. Complete as back and front. Join tiny corner seams.
Welts: With 3¼mm needles and A k up 129 sts along entire lower edge of back. Work 12 rows k 1, p 1 rib. Cast off ribwise. Finish lower edge of front to match. Join side and sleeve seams.

Chart 2

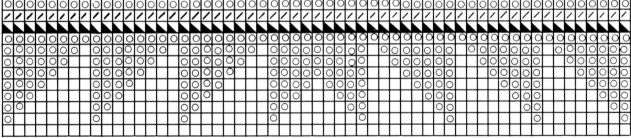

Begin here ▲

KEY FOR CHART 2

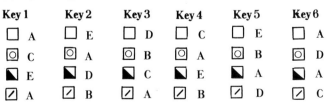

Key 1	Key 2	Key 3	Key 4	Key 5	Key 6
☐ A	☐ E	☐ D	☐ C	☐ E	☐ A
⊡ C	⊡ A	⊡ B	⊡ A	⊡ B	⊡ D
◼ E	◼ D	◼ C	◼ E	◼ A	◼ A
⧄ A	⧄ B	⧄ A	⧄ B	⧄ D	⧄ C

Chart 1

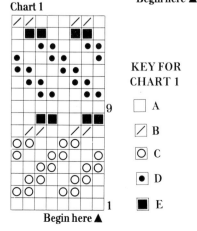

Begin here ▲

KEY FOR CHART 1

☐ A
⧄ B
⊡ C
• D
◼ E

HAT

MATERIALS: Robin Reward DK: 1 (50g) ball each 1st colour wine (A), 2nd colour violet (B), 3rd colour pink (C) and 4th colour green (D); 4mm (No 8) and 3¾mm (No 9) knitting needles; 3·50 crochet hook.
Size: Average.
Tension: 11 sts, 14 rows to 5 cm.
Abbreviations: See page 7.
EAR FLAPS (make 2): With 4mm needles and A cast on 56 sts. **1st row.** With A (k 2 tog, k 24, k 2 tog) twice. **2nd row.** With A k. **3rd row.** With A (k 2 tog, k 22, k 2 tog) twice. **4th row.** As 2nd. Working 2 sts less between decs on next and every alt row, cont in 4-row stripes of B, C, A, B and C. Cast off 8 sts; fold edge in half and join.
MAIN PART: With 3¾mm needles and B cast on 6 sts * beg and ending at cast-on edge of one ear flap k up 38 sts across ends of rows *, cast on 26 sts, rep from * to * again, cast on 6 sts. (114 sts) Work 5 rows g st. Change to 4mm needles. With A, beg k, work 4 rows s st. Cont in s st, working patt from chart thus: Strand A yarn when not in use loosely across wrong side of work, spreading the last few stitches worked to avoid puckering; use a

separate ball of C or D yarn for each diagonal band, stranding colours within band but twisting yarns tog when changing colour at each side of band to avoid holes. Reading 1st and all right side rows from right to left k st before dotted line, rep sts between dotted lines 4 times, k st beyond dotted line; reading 2nd and wrong side rows from left to right p st before dotted line, rep sts between dotted lines 4 times, p st beyond dotted line. Cont until 20 chart rows have been worked. With A work 4 rows. Cont with B and shape top thus: **1st row.** K 1, (k 2 tog, k 24, k 2 tog tbl) 4 times, k 1. **2nd row.** P. **3rd row.** K 1, (k 2 tog, k 22, k 2 tog tbl) 4 times, k 1. **4th row.** P. Cont in this way, working 2 sts less between decs on next and every alt row *at the same time* working 2 rows B, 2 rows C, 4 rows A, 6 rows B, 2 rows C, 4 rows A. **Next row.** With A k 1, (k 2 tog, k 2 tog tbl) 4 times, k 1. Break yarn, thread through sts and fasten off.
MAKING UP: Press work. Join back seam. With A make 2 lengths of 34 ch. Using 20 10-cm lengths of yarn make a B tassel on one end of each cord and on the other end a C tassel; sew B tassels to points of earflaps. Make a B tassel and sew on centre.

Navajo figures

The Navajo formed figures like these in their sandpainting ceremonies. There's more than a touch of magic, too, about this short squared-off sweater in a luxurious mixture of wool and alpaca.

MATERIALS: Jaeger Luxury Spun Double Knitting with Alpaca: 9 (50g) balls main colour grey (A), 1 ball 2nd colour blue (B); Jaeger Matchmaker 2 Double Knitting: 1 (50g) ball each 3rd colour black (C), 4th colour orange (D), 5th colour cream (E) and 6th colour yellow (F); 3¼mm (No 10) and 4mm (No 8) knitting needles.
Measurements: To fit 81 to 102 cm, 32 to 40 inch bust loosely – actual meas, 121 cm; length, 47 cm; sleeve, 39 cm.
Tension: 21 sts, 25 rows to 10 cm.
Abbreviations: See page 7.
Note. – When working chart 1 pattern (see page 108), strand yarn not in use loosely across wrong side of work to avoid puckering. When working chart 2 pattern (see page 108) do not strand yarns but use separate small balls for each block of colour, twisting yarns together on wrong side of work to avoid holes.
BACK: With 3¼mm needles and A cast on 117 sts. Work 8 rows g st. Change to 4mm needles. **Inc row.** P 9, * pick up strand lying between needles and p it tbl – referred to as m 1, p 9; rep from * to end. (129 sts) Cont in s st working patt from chart 1 thus: **1st row** (right side). Reading 1st row of chart from right to left k 5 sts before right-hand dotted line, rep 8 sts between dotted lines to last 4 sts, k 4 sts beyond left-hand dotted line. **2nd row.** Reading 2nd row of chart from left to right p 4 sts before left-hand dotted line, rep 8 sts between

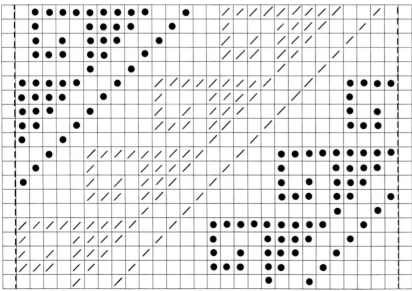

Begin here ▲

☐ A
● C
⊘ D

Chart 2

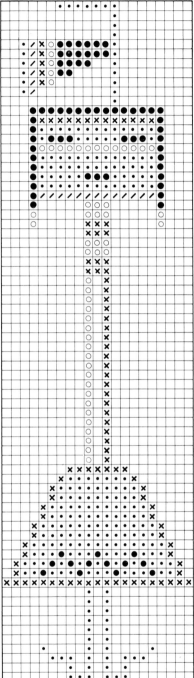

Begin here ▲

Chart 1

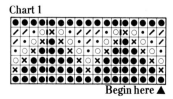

Begin here ▲

A   B   C   D   E   F

dotted lines to last 5 sts, p 5 sts beyond right-hand dotted line. Cont working chart until 7th row has been worked. With A work 3 rows s st. Now work patt from chart 2 thus: **1st row** (right side). * K 4 A, reading 1st row of chart from right to left k 21 sts; rep from * 4 times more, k 4 A. **2nd row.** * P 4 A, reading 2nd row of chart from left to right p 21 sts; rep from * 4 times more, p 4 A. Cont working each chart row until 72nd row has been worked. Work 2 rows s st in A. Now work 7 rows of chart 1 as before **. Cont with A only and work 13 rows s st.

Neck Shaping: Next row. K 50, turn. Cont on these sts only. Cast off 8 sts at beg of next row and 4 sts at beg of foll alt row. Dec 1 st at neck edge on next 3 rows. (35 sts) Work 1 row. Cast off. Sl centre 29 sts on a st-holder, rejoin yarn at inner end of rem sts and work other side to match.

FRONT: As back to **. Cont with A only and work 3 rows s st.

Neck Shaping: Next row. K 58, turn. Cont on these sts only. Cast off 6 sts at beg of next row and 3 sts at beg of foll 2 alt rows. Dec 1 st at neck edge on next 11 rows. (35 sts) Work 1 row. Cast off. Sl centre 13 sts on a st-holder, rejoin yarn at inner end of rem sts and work other side to match.

SLEEVES: With 3¼mm needles and A cast on 43 sts. Work 8 rows g st. Change to 4mm needles. **Inc row.** * P 6, m 1; rep from * 5 times more, p 7. (49 sts) Cont in s st and work 7 rows of chart 1. With A only cont in s st, inc 1 st each end of next and foll 35 alt rows. (121 sts) While working 7 rows of chart 1 cont to inc on every alt row until there are 127 sts. Work 7 rows s st with A. Cast off.

NECKBAND: Join right shoulder seam. With right side facing, using 3¼mm needles and A k up 26 sts down left side of front, k sts from st-holder, k up 26 sts up right side of front, 15 sts down right side of back, k back neck sts, k up 15 sts up left side of back. (124 sts) K 3 rows. **Next row.** K 2 tog, k 62, k 3 tog, k 55, k 2 tog. K 3 rows. **Next row.** K 2 tog, k 60, k 3 tog, k 53, k 2 tog. K 3 rows. **Next row.** K 2 tog, k 58, k 3 tog, k 51, k 2 tog. Cast off knitwise.

MAKING UP: Press lightly. Join left shoulder and neckband seam. Beg and ending 30 cm from shoulder seams, sew sleeves on sides of back and front. Join side and sleeve seams. Press seams.

Sioux arrow-head

This sweater is knitted mostly in the round – the traditional way to create a circular yoke – but the patterns have a rich, primitive effect.

MATERIALS: 3 Suisses Lorena DK: 8 (9) 50g balls main colour brown (A), 2 (3) balls 2nd colour maroon (B), 2 balls each 3rd colour black (C), 4th colour white (D) and 5th colour gold (E); 3¾mm (No 9) and 4mm (No 8) circular knitting needles, 80 cm long; one set each of four 3¾mm (No 9) and 4mm (No 8) double-pointed knitting needles.

Measurements: To fit 81 to 86 (91 to 97) cm, 32 to 34 (36 to 38) inch bust – actual meas, 95 (105) cm; length, 65 (67) cm; sleeve, 44 cm.

Tension: 19 sts, 26 rows to 10 cm.

Abbreviations: See page 7.

Note. – When working multi-colour patterns, do not use the weaving method but strand yarns not in use loosely across wrong side of work to avoid puckering.

MAIN PART: With 3¾mm circular needle and B cast on 180 (200) sts. Marking beg of rounds with loop of contrast thread, cont in rounds and work 7 cm k 1, p 1 rib. Change to 4mm circular needle. Still working in rounds, cont in s st (every round k) working 18-row patt from chart 1 (see page 110) thus: Reading chart from right to left, beg 1st size at 1st dotted line and 2nd size at 2nd dotted line and work 15 (10) sts of 1st row of chart to left, rep complete chart 8 (9)

Chart 2

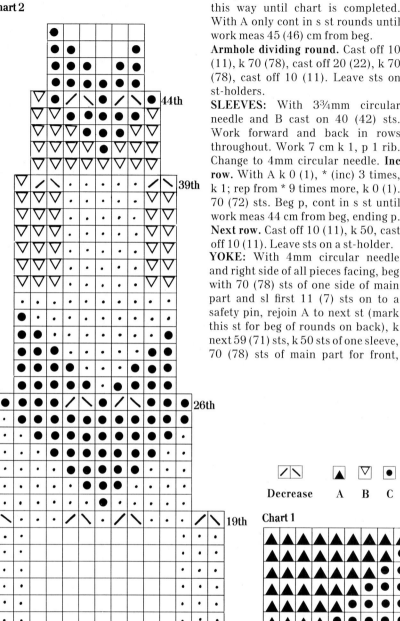

times, then work 5 (10) sts to 1st (2nd) dotted line. Work each round in this way until chart is completed. With A only cont in s st rounds until work meas 45 (46) cm from beg.

Armhole dividing round. Cast off 10 (11), k 70 (78), cast off 20 (22), k 70 (78), cast off 10 (11). Leave sts on st-holders.

SLEEVES: With 3¾mm circular needle and B cast on 40 (42) sts. Work forward and back in rows throughout. Work 7 cm k 1, p 1 rib. Change to 4mm circular needle. **Inc row.** With A k 0 (1), * (inc) 3 times, k 1; rep from * 9 times more, k 0 (1). 70 (72) sts. Beg p, cont in s st until work meas 44 cm from beg, ending p. **Next row.** Cast off 10 (11), k 50, cast off 10 (11). Leave sts on a st-holder.

YOKE: With 4mm circular needle and right side of all pieces facing, beg with 70 (78) sts of one side of main part and sl first 11 (7) sts on to a safety pin, rejoin A to next st (mark this st for beg of rounds on back), k next 59 (71) sts, k 50 sts of one sleeve, 70 (78) sts of main part for front,

50 sts of other sleeve, then k 11 (7) sts from safety pin. 240 (256) sts. K 1 (3) rounds A. Cont in s st rounds working patt from chart 2 (see page 110) thus: Reading from right to left, beg with 1st row of chart and rep 16 sts of chart 15 (16) times for each round until 18th round has been worked. **19th round.** With E * (k 2 tog shown by symbol on chart, k 3, k 2 tog shown by symbol, k 1) twice; rep from * 14 (15) times. 180 (192) sts. Rep 12 sts of reduced width of chart and patt 6 rounds. Change to set of 4mm needles when necessary and work sts k 2 tog as shown by symbols in appropriate colours on next and every numbered round and rep sts of reduced width of chart after each dec round until chart is completed. 90 (96) sts. With D k 2 rounds. Change to set of 3¾mm needles. With B rib 7 cm as given for welt of main part. Cast off loosely rib-wise.

MAKING UP: Do not press. Join sleeve seams. Join underarm seams. Fold neckband in half to wrong side and catch stitch.

Decrease   A   B   C   D   E

Chart 1

Apache thunderbird

Choose rich, earthy colours for a sweater with a bold motif bordered with chevrons.

MATERIALS: Sunbeam Pure New Wool DK: 10 (11:12) 50g balls main colour brick (A), 2 (2:3) balls 2nd colour gold (B), 1 (2:2) balls 3rd colour beige (C) and 1 ball 4th colour blue (D); 3mm (No 11), 3¾mm (No 9) and 4mm (No 8) knitting needles.

Measurements: To fit 81 to 86 (91 to 97:102 to 107) cm, 32 to 34 (36 to 38:40 to 42) inch bust – actual meas, 98 (110:122) cm; length, 61 (62:63) cm; sleeve, 49 (50:51) cm.

Tension: 23 sts, 30 rows to 10 cm over s st using 3¾mm needles.

Abbreviations: See page 7.

Note. – When working multi-colour patterns, use separate balls of yarn for each block of colour, twisting yarns together on wrong side when changing colour to avoid holes.

BACK: With 3mm needles and A cast on 113 (127:141) sts. Work 24 rows k 1, p 1 rib. Change to 4mm needles. Cont in s st working patt from chart 1 (see below) thus: **1st row** (right side). Reading 1st row of chart from right to left k st before dotted line, rep 7 sts beyond dotted line to end. **2nd row.**

Reading 2nd row of chart from left to right rep 7 sts before dotted line to last st, p st beyond dotted line. Cont working each row of chart until all 10 rows have been worked, then work first 5 rows again. Change to 3¾mm needles. With A work 23 (25:27) rows s st. Now work patt from chart 2 (see page 112) thus: **1st row** (right side). K 21 (28:35) A, reading 1st row of chart from left to right k across 36 sts, now beg at dotted line and reading back from right to left k 35 sts, then k 21 (28:35) A. **2nd row.** P 21 (28:35) A, reading 2nd row of chart from left to right p 36 sts, now beg at dotted line and reading back from right to left p across 35 sts, then p 21 (28:35) A. Cont until all 105 chart rows have been worked noting that the beak on rows 86 to 97 should only be worked on left-hand side of head and these sts worked with A on right-hand side **. Cont with A only and work 13 (15:17) rows s st.

Neck Shaping: Next row. K 46 (52:58), turn. Cont on these sts only. Cast off 4 sts at beg of next and foll alt row, then 2 sts at beg of foll alt row. Work 2 rows. Cast off. Sl centre 21 (23:25) sts on a st-holder, rejoin yarn at inner end of rem sts and work other side to match.

FRONT: As back to **. Cont with A only and work 1 (3:5) rows s st.

Neck Shaping: Next row. K 49 (55:61), turn. Cont on these sts only. Cast off 3 sts at beg of next and foll alt row, 2 sts at beg of foll 3 alt rows, then 1 st at beg of foll alt row. Work 8 rows. Cast off. Sl centre 15 (17:19) sts on a st-holder, rejoin yarn and work other side to match.

SLEEVES: With 3mm needles and A cast on 49 sts. Work 29 rows k 1, p 1 rib. **Inc row.** Rib 3, (pick up strand lying between needles and p it tbl –

referred to as m 1, rib 2) 21 times, m 1, rib 4. (71 sts) Change to 4mm needles. While inc 1 st each end of 3rd and every foll 5th (5th:4th) row, beg k, cont in s st and patt 15 rows from chart 1 as back, then change to 3¾mm needles and with A only cont inc as set until there are 113 (113:127) sts. With A work 3 (7:1) rows straight. Change to 4mm needles. Patt 15 rows from chart 1. P 1 row A. Cast off with A.

NECKBAND: Join right shoulder seam. With right side facing, using 3mm needles and A k up 23 sts down left side of front, k sts from st-holder, k up 23 sts up right side of front, 12 sts down right side of back, k back neck sts, k up 12 sts up left side of back. 106 (110:114) sts. Work 7 rows k 1, p 1 rib. Cast off ribwise.

MAKING UP: Press lightly. Join left shoulder and neckband seam. Beg and ending 25 (25:28) cm from shoulder seams, sew sleeves on sides of back and front. Taking half a st into seams, join sides and sleeves.

Chart 1

Begin here ▲

□	◉	⊙
A	B	C

Chart 2

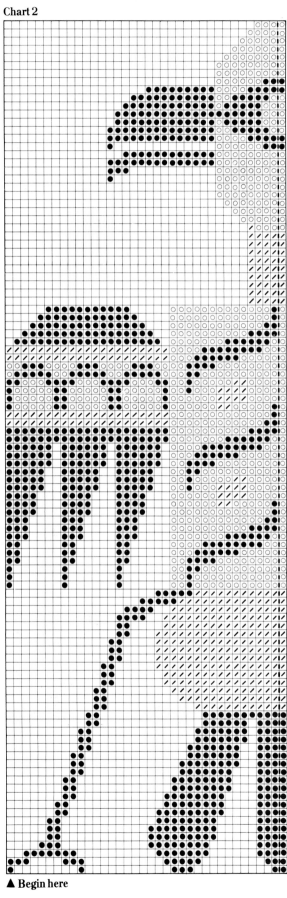

A
● B
○ C
／ D

▲ **Begin here**

Razzle
dazzlers

ophisticated, elegant – and knitted? Yes! If you're painting the town red or looking forward to a candlelit dinner for two, smother yourself in sequins, smoulder in sexy black lace or shrug on a stunning, mohair batwing. You can cover up for cool evenings or show off a summer tan in a vest but in these superb sweaters the night is yours!

STAR SPARKLE

Blue blaze

Smother a simple V neck sweater in sequins for a sophisticated party look.

MATERIALS: Sirdar Wash'n'Wear Crepe is no longer available, we suggest using 6 (7:8) 50g balls Sirdar Country Style for 4 ply knitting; 10 (11:12) strings of knitting sequins obtainable by mail order from Creative Bead Craft Ltd, Denmark Works, Sheepcote Dell Road, Beamond End, Nr Amersham, Bucks, HP7 0RX, tel: 0494 715606, or for personal shoppers from Ells & Farrier Ltd, 20 Princes Street, Hanover Square, London, W1R 8PH, tel: 01-629 9964. 2¾mm (No 12) and 3¼mm (No 10) knitting needles; 2·50 crochet hook.

Measurements: To fit 86 to 91 (91 to 97:97 to 102) cm, 34 to 36 (36 to 38:38 to 40) inch bust – actual meas, 95 (100·5:106) cm; length, 54 (55:56) cm; sleeve, 42 cm.

Tension: 28 sts to 10 cm, 30 rows to 8 cm measured over wrong side.

Abbreviations: See page 7.

Note. – Thread approx 2 strings of sequins on to each of 5 (6:7) balls of yarn. See diagram for threading.

BACK: With 2¾mm needles and unsequinned yarn cast on 122 (129:136) sts. Work 31 rows k 1, p 1 rib. **Inc row.** Rib 7 (6:5), inc, (rib 8, inc) 12 (13:14) times, rib 6 (5:4). 135 (143:151) sts. Change to 3¼mm needles and sequinned yarn. Patt thus: **1st row.** K 3, (insert needle into back of next st and bring a sequin through to front while knitting the st – referred to as s 1, k 3) to end. **2nd row.** P. **3rd row.** K 1, (s 1, k 3) to last 2 sts, s 1, k 1. **4th row.** P. These 4 rows form patt. Cont in patt until work meas 35 cm from beg, ending with a wrong side row.

Armhole Shaping: Cast off 6 sts at beg of next 2 rows. Dec 1 st each end of every row until 107 (111:115) sts rem *. Dec 1 st each end of every alt row until 97 (101:105) sts rem. Cont straight until work meas 54 (55:56) cm, ending with a wrong side row.

Shoulder Shaping: Cast off 9 sts at beg of next 4 rows and 9 (10:11) sts at beg of next 2 rows. Cast off.

FRONT: As back to *.

Neck Shaping: Next row. Patt 53 (55:57) sts, turn. Cont on these sts only. Dec 1 st at each end of next and foll 4 alt rows. Now dec 1 st at neck edge only on *every 3rd row* until 27 (28:29) sts rem. Cont straight for 4 (3:2) rows.

Shoulder Shaping: Cast off 9 sts at beg of next and foll alt row. Work 1 row. Cast off 9 (10:11) sts. Rejoin sequinned yarn; cast off centre st. Complete other side of neck to match.

SLEEVES: With 2¾mm needles and unsequinned yarn cast on 55 (59:63) sts. Beg k, work 5 rows s st. K 1 row (hemline). Change to 3¼mm needles and sequinned yarn. Patt as back, inc 1 st each end of 5th and every foll 6th row until there are 105 (109:113) sts. Patt 9 rows straight. To shape top cast off 6 sts at beg of next 2 rows. Dec 1 st each end of next 5 rows, then dec 1 st each end of every alt row until 51 sts rem. Cast off 3 sts at beg of next 6 rows. Cast off.

MAKING UP: Do not press. Join shoulder seams. Set in sleeves. Join side and sleeve seams. Fold sleeve hems to wrong side at hemline and catch stitch. Join unsequinned yarn to one shoulder and work 1 row double crochet around neck.

THREADING BEADS AND SEQUINS

Sequins are very slightly cupped so thread them with the convex side towards the ball of knitting yarn. Tie a knot in one end of bead or sequin thread so that they can't slip off; tie a loose loop on the other end. Slip end of knitting yarn through this loop and tighten. Slip beads or sequins over on to the knitting yarn. If there is a knot in the knitting yarn, beads or sequins will have to be transferred again to the yarn beyond the knot in the same way. To thread loose beads or sequins on to yarn, twist a short double length of fuse wire around the yarn and use it as a needle.

Double shine

This sequinned vest and beret are worked with metallic yarn to enhance the shimmering, glittering effect.

VEST

MATERIALS: 6 (7:8) 25g balls Twilleys Goldfingering; 13 (14:16) strings of matching knitting sequins (see Blue Blaze for stockist); 3¼mm (No 10) knitting needles.

Measurements: To fit 81 (86 to 91) cm, 32 (34 to 36) inch bust – actual meas, 83 (88:93) cm; length, 40 (40:42) cm; sleeve, 2 cm.

Tension: 15 sts, 26 rows to 5 cm measured on wrong side of work.

Abbreviations: See page 7.

Note. – Thread approximately 2¼ strings of sequins on to each of 5 (6:7) balls of yarn (Blue Blaze diagram), leaving 1 ball unsequinned. Knitted from side to side.

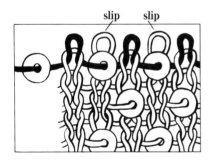

slip   slip

BACK: Beg at sleeve edge. With 3¼mm needles and unsequinned yarn cast on 57 (57:59) sts. Work 4 rows g st. Change to sequinned yarn. Cont in patt thus: **1st row.** K 1, (yfd, sl 1 purlwise, push a sequin up close to front of work, ybk – referred to as s 1, k 1) to end. **2nd row.** P. **3rd row.** K 2, (s 1, k 1) to last st, k 1. **4th row.** P. These 4 rows form patt. Rep them once. Cast on 60 (60:64) sts at

beg of next row for side edge. 117
(117:123) sts*. Work 41·5 (44:46·5)
cm straight, ending p. ** Cast off 60
(60:64) sts at beg of next row. Patt 7
rows. Change to unsequinned yarn
and work 4 rows g st. Cast off.
FRONT: As back to *. Work 10
(10:11) cm, ending with a right side
row.
Neck Shaping: Cast off 12 sts at beg of
next row. Dec 1 st at end of next row
and at same edge on next 5 rows. 99
(99:105) sts. Cont straight until work
meas 30 (32·5:34) cm from cast-on
side edge, ending with a right side
row. Inc 1 st at beg of next row and at
same edge on next 5 rows. Cast on 12
sts at beg of next row. Cont straight
until work meas 41·5 (44:46·5) cm
from cast-on side edge, ending p.
Complete as back from **.
EDGINGS: Work with unsequinned
yarn. With 3¼mm needles k up 116
(123:130) sts along lower edge of
back. Work 4 rows g st. Cast off knitwise. Finish lower edge of front to
match. Join right shoulder. With
3¼mm needles k up 136 (148:152)
sts around neck. Work 2 rows g st.
Cast off knitwise.
MAKING UP: Do not press. Join left
shoulder and neck edging seam. Join
side and tiny sleeve seams.

BERET

MATERIALS: 1 (25g) ball Twilleys
Goldfingering; 2 strings knitting sequins (for stockist see Blue Blaze);
3mm (No 11) and 2¾mm (No 12)
knitting needles.
Size: Average.
Tension: 15 sts, 28 rows to 5 cm.
TO MAKE: Thread sequins on to yarn
(see diagram and note with Blue
Blaze). With 3mm needles cast on 45
sts. * **1st row** (right side). K 1, (s 1 as
given for Vest, k 1) to end. **2nd row.** P.
3rd row. K 2, (s 1, k 1) to last 3 sts,
turn. **4th row.** P. **5th row.** As 1st row
to last 6 sts, turn. **6th row.** P. **7th row.**
As 3rd to last 9 sts, turn. Cont in this
way leaving 3 sts more before turning
on every alt row until row reading: As
3rd row to last 27 sts, turn has been
worked. P 1 row. Rep from * 11 times
more. Cast off.
EDGING: With right side facing,
using 2¾mm needles k up 169 sts
around curved edge. Work 4 rows
g st. Cast off. Join straight edges and
ends of edging.

Pinstripe

The glistening beaded stripes are easy to do because the
vest is knitted sideways. Complete the bell-hop effect
with a saucy pill-box hat.

MATERIALS: *Vest.–* 3 (3:4) 50g
balls Patons Beehive 4 ply; 50g
Silver Bugle Beads No BB2-1 (see
Blue Blaze for stockist); 2 small
buttons. *Hat.–* 1 (50g) ball Patons
Beehive 4 ply; 25g Silver Bugle Beads
No BB2-1; 15 cm diameter circle of
buckram and 48 cm of cardboard,
3 cm wide; 17 cm diameter circle and
strip 50 cm long by 5 cm wide of lining. 2¾mm (No 12) and 3mm (No 11)
knitting needles.
Measurements: *Vest.–* To fit 86
(91:97) cm, 34 (36:38) inch bust
snugly – actual meas, 83 (88:93) cm;
length, 49 (50:51) cm. *Hat.–* 48 cm
circumference.
Tension: 15 sts, 20 rows to 5 cm.
Abbreviations: See page 7.

VEST

Note. – Thread beads (see Blue Blaze
for diagram) on to 1 ball of yarn –
referred to as B yarn; unbeaded yarn
is referred to as A yarn. Carry yarn
not in use loosely up edge of work.
Knitted from side to side.

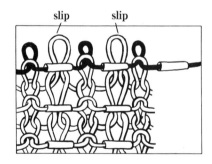

slip   slip

BACK: Beg at right side edge. With
3mm needles and A yarn cast on 69
(71:73) sts. Patt thus: Beg k, work 7
rows s st. **Bead row** (wrong side).
With 2¾mm needle and B yarn k 1,
(with ybk sl next st purlwise, sl bead
up close to work, k 1) to end. **Next
row.** With 3mm needles and B yarn k
to end. Cont with A yarn and p 1 row.

These 10 rows form patt. Patt 4 rows.
Armhole Shaping: Cont in patt, inc 1
st at beg of next row and at this edge
on every foll row until there are 105
(109:113) sts. Cast on 20 sts at beg of
next row *. Patt 29 (33:35) rows
straight.
Back Opening: Cast off 28 sts at beg of
next row. Patt 3 (1:3) rows straight.
Cast on 28 sts at beg of next row. Patt
29 (33:35) rows straight.
Armhole Shaping: ** Cast off 20 sts at
beg of next row, then dec 1 st at this
edge on every row until 69 (71:73) sts
rem. Patt 14 rows straight. Cast off
loosely.
FRONT: Beg at left side edge and
work as back to *. Patt 9 (11:13) rows
straight.
Neck Shaping: Cast off 9 sts at beg of
next row, then dec 1 st at this edge on
next 9 rows. Patt 25 (27:29) rows
straight. Inc 1 st at neck edge on next
9 rows. Cast on 9 sts at beg of next
row. Patt 9 (11:13) rows straight.
Complete as back from ** of armhole
shaping.
NECKBAND: Matching 9 (11:13)
rows of front shoulders to corresponding rows of back, join shoulder
seams. With right side facing, using
2¾mm needles and B yarn k up 17
(18:19) sts across left back, 61
(63:65) sts around front and 17
(18:19) sts across right back. 95
(99:103) sts. *Next row (wrong
side). As bead row. K 1 row. Rep
these 2 rows 7 times more, then rep
bead row again *. Cast off. With right
side facing, using 2¾mm needles and
A yarn, beg and ending at cast-off
edge of neckband k up 66 sts around
back opening. K 1 row. Cast off.
ARMBANDS: With right side facing,
using 2¾mm needles and A yarn k up
128 (132:136) sts around armhole.
K 1 row. Cast off knitwise.
WELTS: With right side facing, using
2¾mm needles and A yarn k up 121
(127:133) sts across lower edge of
back. Work 7 cm k 1, p 1 rib. Cast off
ribwise. Work front welt to match.

MAKING UP: Join side seams. Make 2 button loops on end of neckband; sew on buttons.

PILLBOX HAT

TO MAKE: Thread 630 beads on to yarn (see Blue Blaze for diagram). With 2¾mm needles cast on 141 sts. Work as neckband of vest from * to *.

Crown Shaping: Now with unbeaded yarn, beg k, cont in s st. Dec 1 st at beg of 1st row. P 1 row. **Dec row.** (K 2 tog, k 5) to end. Work 3 rows. **Dec row.** (K 2 tog, k 4) to end. Cont dec on every 4th row in this way, working 1 st less after decs until 40 sts rem. P 1 row. **Dec row.** (K 2 tog) to end. Rep last 2 rows 3 times more. Break yarn, thread end through rem sts, draw up and fasten off securely.

MAKING UP: Join seam. *Hat Shape.*– Turn 1 cm edges of lining circle over buckram circle and sew down. Turn 1 cm edges of lining strip over card and stick down; join ends and sew on around circle, right sides inwards. Stretch knitted fabric over shape and sew cast-on edge around lower edge of lined hat shape. Catch stitch top edge of beaded band through seam of shape.

Black magic

Contrast the softness of kid mohair with plunging V's of lace for a stunning, sexy sweater.

MATERIALS: Scotnord Janine Mohair is no longer available, we suggest using 4 (5:5) 50g balls Emu Kid Mohair; 3mm (No 11) and 3¼mm (No 10) knitting needles; 30 cm black lace, at least 90 cm wide with both selvedges scalloped; 2 m black tape, 5mm wide.

Measurements: To fit 81 (86:91) cm, 32 (34:36) inch bust – actual meas, 81 (86:91) cm; length, 56 (57:58) cm; sleeve, 42 (43:44) cm.

Tension: 12 sts, 16 rows to 5 cm.

Abbreviations: See page 7.

Note. – For ease in counting mark inc and dec rows with contrast yarn.

BACK AND FRONT (alike): With 3mm needles cast on 95 (101 :107) sts. Work 14 rows k 1, p 1 rib. Change to 3¼mm needles. Beg p, cont in rev s st, dec 1 st each end of 1st row and every foll 6th row until 83 (89:95) sts rem. Work 11 rows straight.

Inset Shaping: Next row. Inc in 1st st, k 40 (43:46), turn. Cont on these sts only. While dec 1 st at inset edge on every foll 5th row *at the same time* inc 1 st at side edge on every foll 8th row until 8 incs in all have been worked and there are 38 (41:44) sts. While dec as set at inset edge only, work 13 rows.

Armhole Shaping: Still dec at inset edge, cast off 7 sts at beg of next row, then dec 1 st at beg of 6 (7:8) alt rows. Cont dec at inset edge only until 12 (13:14) sts rem. Work 3 (2:1) rows.

Shoulder Shaping: Cast off 6 (6:7) sts at beg of next row. Work 1 row. Cast off 6 (7:7) sts. Cast off 1 st at centre and work other side to match.

SLEEVES: With 3mm needles cast on 47 (49:51) sts. Work 14 rows rib as back and front. Beg p, cont in rev s st, inc 1 st each end of next and every foll 8th row until there are 75 (79:83) sts. Work 15 (11:7) rows straight. To shape top cast off 7 sts at beg of next 2 rows. Dec 1 st each end of next row and foll 6 (7:8) alt rows. Dec 1 st each end of every 4th row until 39 (41:43) sts rem. Dec 1 st each end of every alt row until 29 sts rem. Work 1 row. Cast off 2 sts at beg of next 8 rows. Cast off.

NECK EDGING: With right side of back or front facing, using 3mm needles, beg at shoulder and k up 96 sts down shaped inset edge to point of V, 1 st from centre and 96 sts up other side to shoulder. Cast off knitwise. Work other side to match.

MAKING UP: Do not press. *For Lace Inset.* – On paper enlarge triangle shape shown in diagram to measurements given. With top edge of paper pattern to outer rim of scalloped edge and centre of top edge to centre of a scallop, pin on and tack around both sides of V outline. Machine stitch or back stitch just outside this line. Remove tacking. On wrong side of lace, pin tape just outside stitching line around both sides of V. Tack in place without puckering. Overlock or herring-bone stitch down centre of tape through on to lace. Cut out lace close to tape. Work another piece to match. Beg and ending 2 cm down from cast-off edge of shoulders, with right side of lace and knitting upwards, tack lace under edging of knitting so that cast-off edge overlaps stitching line of lace. Machine stitch or back stitch within cast-off edge. Join shoulders. Set in sleeves. Join side and sleeve seams.

21 (22:23)

10·5 (11:11·5)

38 (39:40)

Measurements given in centimetres

Neon lights

Electric squiggles light up this huge batwing sweater. Knitted in mohair, it's the perfect cover-up at night.

MATERIALS: Jaeger Mohair-Spun is no longer available, we suggest using Jaeger Mohair Gold: 8 (50g) balls main colour black (A), 1 ball each 2nd colour red (B) and 3rd-colour green (C); 5mm (No 6) and 6mm (No 4) knitting needles.

Measurements: To fit 86 to 97 cm, 34 to 38 inch bust – actual meas around batwing at underarm, 148 cm; length, 69 cm; sleeve, 39 cm.

Tension: 16 sts, 19 rows to 10 cm.

Abbreviations: See page 7.

Note. – When working multi-colour pattern, do not strand yarns across work but use a separate ball of yarn for each block of colour and twist yarns together on wrong side when changing colour to avoid holes.

FRONT: With 5mm needles and A cast on 72 sts. Work 5 cm k 1, p 1 rib. Change to 6mm needles and k 1 row *. Cont in s st working patt from chart 1 (see note), reading p rows from left to right and k rows from right to left thus: **1st chart row.** P 52 A, 10 B, 10 A. **2nd chart row.** K 7 A, 4 B, 7 A, 2 B, 52 A. **3rd chart row.** P 51 A, 2 B, 11 A, 5 B, 3 A. **4th chart row.** With A inc in 1st st, k 3 B, 15 A, 2 B, 50 A, inc in last st. Cont working from chart 1 as set, inc 1 st each end of every 3rd row (as shown by stepped edge of chart) until there are 120 sts. Work 12 rows straight, ending p **.

Raglan and Neck Shaping: Dec 1 st each end of next 2 rows. **Next row.** K 2 tog, k 54, k 2 tog, turn. Cont with A on these sts only. Dec 1 st each end of every row until 32 sts rem. Still shaping raglan on every row, dec 1 st at neck edge on every alt row until 2 sts rem. Take 2 tog and fasten off. With right side facing, rejoin yarn to

inner end of rem sts and still working patt from chart as set, complete as 1st side, reversing neck and raglan shapings.

BACK: As front to *. Reading p rows from right to left and k rows from left to right to reverse patt, cont thus: **1st chart row.** P 10 A, 10 B, 52 A. **2nd chart row.** K 52 A, 2 B, 7 A, 4 B, 7 A. Cont in patt as set, working as given for front to **.

Raglan Shaping: Still working from chart as set, dec 1 st each end of every row until 50 sts rem. **Next row.** (K 4, k 2 tog) 8 times, k 2. (42 sts) Cast off loosely.

RIGHT SLEEVE: With 5mm needles and A cast on 32 sts. Work 5 cm k 1, p 1 rib. Change to 6mm needles. Cont in s st, inc 1 st each end of 4th and

every foll 3rd row until there are 62 sts. K 1 row. Now work from chart 2 as given for chart 1 for front thus: **1st chart row.** P 37 A, 4 B, 21 A. Cont working from chart 2 as set *at the same time* inc 1 st each end of next and every foll 3rd row until there are 70 sts. Work 6 rows straight. To shape raglan cont working from chart 2 while dec 1 st each end of every row until chart is completed, then cont with A only until 6 sts rem. Dec 1 st each end of foll 2 alt rows. Take 2 tog and fasten off.

LEFT SLEEVE: As right sleeve but omit patt and work with A throughout.

NECKBAND: Join both front and right back raglan seams. With right side facing, using 5mm needles and A

Chart 1

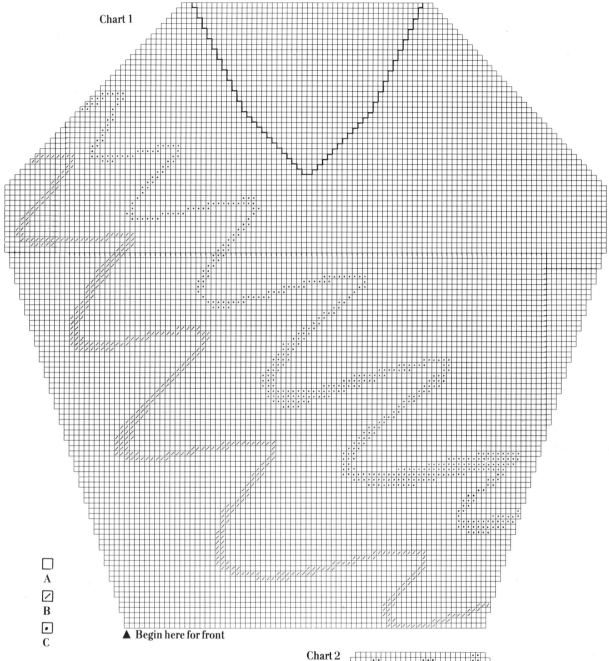

▲ **Begin here for front**

A
B
C

Chart 2

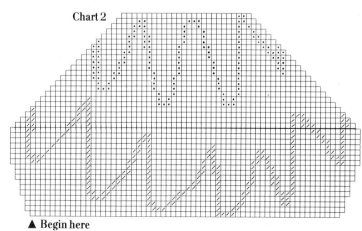

▲ **Begin here**

k up 1 st from top of left sleeve, 36 sts down left side of front neck, 1 st from centre V, 36 sts up right side of front neck, 1 st from top of right sleeve and 42 sts across back neck. (117 sts) **1st row.** P 1, (k 1, p 1) to within 2 sts of centre st, k 2 tog, p centre st, k 2 tog tbl, (p 1, k 1) to last st, p 1. Dec 1 st each side of centre front st on every row, work 4 more rows in rib as set. Cast off ribwise.

MAKING UP: Press very lightly. Join left back raglan and neckband seam. Join side and sleeve seams. Press seams very lightly.

Star sparkle

Swirling stars cascade over this long sweater.

MATERIALS: Avocet Soirée Lurex Chainette: 14 (50g) spools main colour Black Silver (A) and 1 spool each 2nd colour Silver Sparkle (B), 3rd colour Yellow Gold (C). Avocet Soirée Chainette: 2 (50g) spools 4th colour red (D) and 1 spool 5th colour purple (E); 4mm (No 8) and 6mm (No 4) knitting needles; shoulder pads.

Measurements: To fit 86 to 97 cm, 34 to 38 inch bust – actual meas, 111 cm; length, 69 cm; sleeve, 44 cm.
Tension: 18 sts, 26 rows to 10 cm.
Abbreviations: See page 7.
Note. – Cut ends of yarn across diagonally to prevent fraying. When working multi-colour motif do not strand yarns, but use a separate small ball for each block of colour, twisting yarns together when changing colour to avoid holes. Centre area of chart enclosed by dotted lines is area of pattern to be knitted (28 stitches and 34 rows referred to throughout instructions). Pattern area of chart beyond dotted lines is embroidered in Swiss Darning over finished work.
BACK: With 4mm needles and A cast on 102 sts. Work 8 rows k 1, p 1 rib. Change to 6mm needles. Beg k, work 8 rows s st. Cont in s st working patt from chart thus: **Next row** (beg 1st motif). K 67 A, reading centre area of chart from right to left k 28 sts of 1st row, k 7 A. **Next row.** P 7 A, reading

centre area of chart from left to right p 28 sts of 2nd row, p 67 A. Cont in this way until 22nd chart row has been worked. **Next row** (beg 2nd motif). K 9 A, k 28 sts of 1st row of chart, k 30 A, k 28 sts of 23rd row of chart, k 7 A. **Next row.** P 7 A, p 28 sts of 24th row of chart, p 30 A, p 28 sts of 2nd row of chart, p 9 A. Cont in this way until 1st motif has been completed, then cont in s st with A over these 28 sts until 34th chart row of 2nd motif has been worked. With A work 2 rows. **Next row** (beg 3rd motif). K 56 A, k 28 sts of 1st row of chart, k 18 A. Cont in this way until 30th chart row of 3rd motif has been worked. **Next row** (beg 4th motif). K 13 A, k 28 sts of 1st row of chart, k 15 A, k 28 sts of 31st row of chart, k 18 A. Patt 3 rows, completing 3rd motif.
Armhole Shaping: Cont in patt as set, casting off 4 sts at beg of next 2 rows. Patt until 26th chart row of 4th motif has been worked. **Next row** (beg 5th motif). K 9 A, k 28 sts of 27th chart row, k 25 A, k 28 sts of 1st chart row, k 4 A **. Cont in this way until 34th chart row of 5th motif has been worked. With A only work 16 rows.
Shoulder Shaping: Cast off 23 sts at beg of next 2 rows. Cast off rem 48 sts.
FRONT: As back to **. Cont until 14th chart row of 5th motif has been worked.
Neck Shaping: Next row. K 47 A, turn. Cont with A only. Dec 1 st at neck edge on next 2 rows; work 1 row straight. Rep last 3 rows until 23 sts rem. Cast off. Rejoin yarn to inner end of rem sts, k 15 A, patt 28 sts of 15th chart row, k 4 A. Work to match other side, reversing shaping and after completing 5th motif, working with A only.
SLEEVES: With 4mm needles and A cast on 46 sts. Work 8 rows k 1, p 1 rib. Change to 6mm needles. Beg k, cont in s st, working patt from chart thus: **1st row** (beg 1st motif). With A inc, k 10, k 28 sts of 1st chart row, with A k 6, inc. Cont in patt, inc 1 st each end of every foll 4th row until 34th chart row of 1st motif has been worked. Still inc as set work 14 rows A. (70 sts) **Next row** (beg 2nd motif). With A inc, k 2, k 28 sts of 1st chart row, with A k 38, inc. Still inc, cont until 16th chart row of 2nd motif has been worked. (78 sts) **Next row** (beg 3rd motif). With A inc, k 6, k 28 sts of 17th chart row, k 16 A, k 26 sts of 1st chart row, inc in 27th st of chart. **Next**

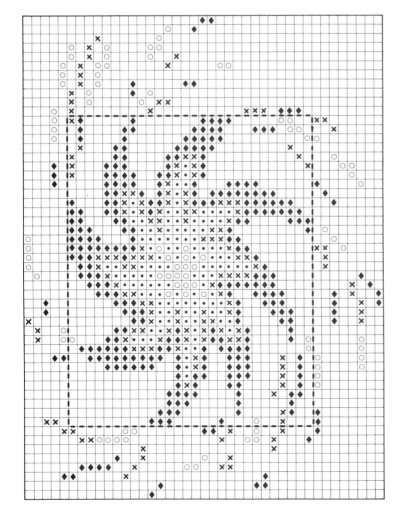

A
B
C
D
E

row. P 28 sts of 2nd chart row, p 16 A, p 28 sts of 18th chart row, p 8 A. Cont in patt, inc as set until 3rd motif has been completed. (96 sts) Cont with A only, inc until there are 100 sts. Work 7 rows A. Cast off loosely.

NECK EDGING: Join right shoulder seam. With 4mm needles and A k up 40 sts down left side of front, 1 st from centre of V, 40 sts up right side of front, 48 sts across back neck. (129 sts) **1st row.** K to within 2 sts of centre st, k 2 tog, k 1, k 2 tog, k to end. While dec 1 st each side of centre st as before *at the same time* cast off.

MAKING UP: *Embroidery.* – Around each knitted motif on back and front, Swiss Darn sts as shown in border around knitting chart. On sleeves omit lower border on 1st motif and adjust embroidered area at outer edges of 2nd and 3rd motifs. Join left shoulder and neck edging seam. Setting 2 cm at sides of sleeves to cast off edges at underarm, set in sleeves. Join side and sleeve seams. Sew in shoulder pads.

Spinners
and yarn suppliers

If you have difficulty in obtaining yarn for any of the
garments featured in this book please write, enclosing
an sae to the yarn company named in the materials at the
address opposite. In just a few cases the yarn originally
featured in *Woman* magazine is no longer made. Rather
than leave out some of our – and your – favourite
designs, we have given a satisfactory substitute in the
materials so that all yarns featured in this book are
available at the time of going to press.

Argyll Wools Ltd
PO Box 15
Priestley Mills
Pudsey
West Yorkshire LS28 9LT
Tel: 0532 558411

Avocet Hand Knitting Yarns
Hammond Associates Ltd
Hammerain House
Hookstone Avenue
Harrogate
North Yorkshire HG2 8ER
Tel: 0423 871440

The Cambrian Factory
Llanwrtyd Wells
Powys LD5 4SD
Tel: 059 13211

Coats
Marketing Services Dept
39 Durham Street
Glasgow G41 1BS
Tel: 041-427 5311

Emu Wools Ltd
Customer Service
Leeds Road
Greengates
Bradford
West Yorkshire BD10 9TE
Tel: 0274 614031

The Handweavers' Studio
29 Haroldstone Road
London E17 7AN
Tel: 01-521 2281

Hayfield Textiles Ltd
Hayfield Mills
Glusburn
Nr Keighley
West Yorkshire BD20 8QP
Tel: 0535 33333

Jaeger Hand Knitting Ltd
Alloa
Clackmannanshire
Scotland FK10 1EG
Tel: 0259 723431

Jamieson and Smith (SWB) Ltd
90 North Road
Lerwick
Shetland Isles ZE1 0PQ
Tel: 0595 3579

King Cole Ltd
Merrie Mills
Old Souls Way
Bingley
West Yorkshire BD16 2AX
Tel: 0274 561331

Lister Handknitting
Whiteoak Mills
Westgate
Wakefield
West Yorkshire WF2 9SF
Tel: 0924 375311

Patons & Baldwins Ltd
Alloa
Clackmannanshire
Scotland FK10 1EG
Tel: 0259 723431

Phildar (UK) Ltd
4 Gambrel Road
Westgate Industrial Estate
Northampton NN5 5NF
Tel: 0604 583111

Pingouin
French Wools
7/11 Lexington Street
London W1R 4BU
Tel: 01-439 8891

Richard Poppleton and Sons
Albert Mills
Horbury
Wakefield
West Yorkshire WF4 5NJ
Tel: 0924 264141

Robin Wools Ltd
Robin Mills
Idle
Bradford
West Yorkshire BD10 9TE
Tel: 0274 612561

Rowan Yarns
Green Lane Mill
Washpit
Holmfirth
West Yorkshire HD7 1RW
Tel: 0484 687714

Schachenmayr
PPT Yarns
Ambergate
Derby DE5 2EY
Tel: 077 385 2469

Scotnord Ltd
PO Box 27
Athey Street
Macclesfield
Cheshire SK11 8EA
Tel: 0625 29436/7/8

Sirdar plc
Consumer Service Dept
Flanshaw Lane
Alverthorpe
Wakefield
West Yorkshire WF2 9ND
Tel: 0924 371501

Studio Yarns Ltd
The Citadel
Blenheim Gardens
London SW2 5EU
Tel: 01-671 7626

3 Suisses
9 King Street
Leicester LE1 6RN
Tel: 0533 554713

Sunbeam Knitting Wools
Crawshaw Mills
Pudsey
West Yorkshire LS28 7BS
Tel: 0532 571871

Tootal Knit Yarns
Tootal Craft
56 Oxford Street
Manchester M60 1HJ
Tel: 061-228 0474

H. G. Twilley Ltd
Roman Mill
Stamford
Lincolnshire PE9 1BG
Tel: 0780 52661

Viking Wools Ltd
Rothay Holme
Rothay Road
Ambleside
Cumbria LA22 0HQ
Tel: 0966 32991

Wendy Wools
Carter & Parker Ltd
Guisely
Leeds
West Yorkshire LS20 9PD
Tel: 0943 72264

Acknowledgements

The photographs featured on the following pages were taken by:

Belinda 25, 35.
Tony Boase 6, 15, 16, 17, 19, 31, 51, 53, 70, 71, 83, 86, 87, 89, 94, 95, 107, 109, 111, 113, 122.
Nick Briggs front cover, 99, 101, 103, 104, 116.
Roger Charity 11, 12, 13.
Jill Green and Neil Phillips of Pinsharp 63, 65, 67, 69, 73, 74, 76, 77, 85, 91, 92, 115, 125.
Chris Grout Smith 37, 50.
Heinz Lautenbacher 9, 20, 23, 32, 33, 79, 80, 117, 119.
Eamonn J. McCabe 44, 45, 61, 97.
Francesca Sullivan 27, 28, 30, 39, 43, 54, 58, 120, 121, back cover.

The designs featured in this book include work by the following designers:

Gaye Bocock 49, 78, 88, 92.
Jeanette Boyle 14.
Kate Butcher 111.
Jenny Causer 108.
Anne Chapman 124.
Tina Clarke 22.
Karen Colley 106.
Tessa Dennison 18.
Melody Griffiths 36, 59, 100, 105.
Nadine Hobro 76.
Caroline Ingram 62, 72, 74.
Mary Norden 17, 71, 86.
Pat Quiroga 10, 11, 29, 31, 32, 93, 118.
Betty Speller 26.
Lesley Stanfield 16, 21, 87, 102, 106, 117.
Kate Strachan 95.
Aileen Swan 28, 38, 81, 82, 90, 120.
Jane Taylor 44, 55.
Sue Turton 96.

Instructions re-written by Aileen Swan
Charts re-drawn by Kate Strachan
Checking by Aileen Swan, Kate Strachan, Shirley Bradford and Melody Griffiths

Designed by Graham Davis Associates
Designer Kevin Ryan
Typesetter Dawkins